AS for
AQA

success in
sociology

Teacher's Guide

Peter Covington   **Vicki Piper**

© 2008 Folens Limited, on behalf of the author

United Kingdom: Folens Publishers, Waterslade House, Thame Road, Haddenham, Buckinghamshire, HP17 8NT

Email: folens@folens.com

Ireland: Folens Publishers, Greenhills Road, Tallaght, Dublin 24

Email: info@folens.ie

Editor: Joanne Murray

Design and layout: eMC Design

Cover design: Jump To!

First published 2008 by Folens Limited

British Cataloguing in Publication Data. A catalogue record for this publication is available from the British Library.

ISBN 978-1-85008-261-3

Folens code: FD2613

Contents

Lesson plans for Topic Six: Sociological methods   82

Introduction

Sociology is a very popular subject in schools and colleges. As few schools offer the subject at GCSE, it is probable that most AS students will be completely new to the subject.

It is also likely that, as a teacher, Sociology is not the only subject you teach. I completed my PGCE with the sole intention of teaching Sociology, yet have found myself also teaching Psychology, Health and Social Care, Literacy and Key Skills over the years. Sociology is frequently added as a second subject in job vacancies, so that requests for a teacher of Psychology with Sociology, or even Geography with Sociology are not uncommon.

Whether you are an experienced sociology specialist, an NQT commencing your first post, or a non-specialist taking up sociology as an additional subject, this teacher's guide aims to meet your needs. Lesson by lesson plans are provided in detail for every topic within the new AQA specification. The lesson plans follow the order of both the specification and the *Folens AS Student Book*, and include a wealth of student-centred activities, links to useful websites and other tips for helping your students achieve their potential. Suggested homework activities are also provided.

Planning your programme of study

If you are new to teaching, or to using AQA as the examining board for sociology, choosing which modules to teach and when to teach them can seem daunting. The good news is that you do not need to teach all six topics unless you want to! Indeed, many centres choose to teach the minimum amount of topics needed. The options are as follows:

Topic One (SCLY1) worth 40 per cent of the overall AS grade:
- *Culture and identity* (which is a completely new topic area), or
- *Families and households*, or
- *Wealth, poverty and welfare*

Topic Two (SCLY2) worth 60 per cent of the overall AS grade:
- A compulsory *research methods* section, plus
- *Education and research methods in education*, or
- *Health and research methods in health*

So, it would be quite acceptable to only teach *families and households*, *education* (including research methods in context) and *sociological methods*, for example.

The decision on how many topics to offer your students will largely depend on time constraints. Whilst some schools and colleges allow five hours per week to deliver A level subjects, others allow as little as three hours. And, of course, there is the 'depth versus breadth' debate: is it better to teach one topic in considerable depth, or give your students the choice of two exam topics to choose from, but spend less time on each?

You may also have to decide whether to enter your students for the January examination. Both SCLY1 and SCLY2 are available in January and June. If you will be able to finish an entire module during the autumn term, it may be a wise decision for your students to sit an exam in January, thus reducing the pressure come June.

Resources

In addition to this teacher book, Folens has produced a corresponding student book. Used together they should provide you with a comprehensive set of resources to teach AS Sociology.

How these resources achieve the best results for your students

In writing this material I had a number of objectives. Firstly, to write a student book that meets the needs of a wide range of students, that is informative, authoritative, but not pompous. I have written it to appeal to all students, whether they expect to achieve an A grade or an E grade in their terminal examination. You will notice that although I use appropriate terminology where necessary, I have tried to give examples as often as possible to explain theories. This allows students to learn sociological language and terminology as they progress through the text.

Secondly, to create a teacher's guide that will be of daily use. This resource is designed specifically with the teacher in mind.

The structure of the student book

The student book is designed specifically to tie in with the new 2009 AQA Sociology Specification. It has been written to meet the requirements of the spec, and developed to help integrate the core components within your teaching. To help achieve this I have designed a number of activities that particularly focus on theory and methods, thereby ensuring students see this area of sociology as being integral to their understanding.

While the book closely follows the new specification, it is intended to provide a relevant and contemporary resource providing a basis for student success, whilst also assisting the teacher in delivering this. The text therefore closely follows the specification, with each module being subdivided into section areas. It covers all of the six topics covered in the new specification. The book also offers a number of options for students. So for example, it can be used by students doing Health and Social Care, as well as those sitting AS Sociology.

The structure of the teacher's guide

There is a scheme of work for each topic, followed by a set of lesson plans. The lesson plans are structured with the following sections:

- **Start positive:** An alternative to starting your lessons with 'stop talking please'!
- **Connect learning:** A set of questions that test students' knowledge based on the previous lesson.
- **Share learning objectives:** Tells students exactly what they need to achieve during the lesson.
- **Lesson outline:** Summarises what you will be teaching in a single sentence.
- **Starter hook:** Usually a short but fun activity to get students thinking about the topic, and leave them wanting more!
- **Activities:** Activities vary in length and range from research tasks to role plays.
- **Review learning:** The lesson plenary, in which students are tested on what they have learned.
- **Preview next lesson:** A look at what students can expect in their next lesson.
- **End positively:** Ways to praise your class.
- **What the examiners are looking for:** Shows how the lesson ties in with the spec and what the questions might look like in the exam.
- **Homework:** Gives you ideas for setting homework to the students.
- **Getting the most out of your class:** A range of tips and suggestions to motivate and inspire your students.

You will notice that the lesson plans do not include suggested timings. These have been purposely omitted due to teachers using different amounts of time to complete each section. Therefore, whilst some teachers may only be able to spend one hour on each lesson plan, the activities are flexible enough that other teachers may divide one lesson into three 45 minute slots.

Teaching the new specification

The new AQA AS Sociology specification was developed in response to the 2005 Review of Curriculum 2000. Essentially, the new specification maintains continuity with the current specification, allowing teachers to continue to teach the same modules as the present specification (although the *work and leisure* option is no longer available, and *mass media* is now an A2 topic). As before, the specification offers students the option of choosing AS Sociology without having previously studied GCSE Sociology. Furthermore, in response to student complaints about the number of modules they had to sit, the new specification is reduced from six modules (AS and A2) to four modules.

Changes that have occurred to the specification have been introduced to ensure that AS Sociology stays contemporary. So, for example, new areas of sociology, such as globalisation, have been included. Additionally, areas that have been used by students to answer questions have also been added. Much else remains unchanged. The one real difference between the present specification and the new one lies in the absence of coursework.

Consequently, AQA have decided to introduce *methods in context* within Topics Two and Four. What is meant by this is that, in addition to a section of the exam dedicated to sociological methods, there is also an essay question linking the use of sociological research methods to the study of education or health. Practically, this means that teachers will have to modify their teaching to allow 'mini projects' on substantive areas within the Topic Two module (education or health). This has the advantage that you can combine theory and methods as an integral part of your teaching. With the time that has been freed up from the loss of two modules, there should be sufficient time for this exploration.

According to the board, the underlying principles of the new specification are to offer candidates sufficient time in the exams to demonstrate their knowledge. On this point, it is interesting to note that although there are fewer modules, the actual examination time is little changed.

Teaching A levels: the golden rules

- Demonstrate your own enjoyment of the subject.
- Be well prepared. For example, give out a summary of your scheme of work before you start each section. This allows the students to tick off each section area as they finish it, but it also means that they can do research before they cover a new section with you.

- Prepare your lessons and keep them contemporary. Sociology is an active subject: almost as soon as you put statistics or studies in front of your students they are out of date.
- Engage your students in discussion. Talking is an excellent way of engaging your students and diagnosing any weaknesses in their knowledge.

Leading on from the above, one of the most important factors for successful teaching is questioning. Again and again OFSTED inspectors comment that effective questioning is vital for effective progress. What this means is asking a combination of appropriate open and closed questions during lesson time.

Question at the start of the lesson: Research shows that people are more likely to remember the first and last things that are said to them. This is called the recency effect. Therefore an excellent way of getting students to learn is to test them at the start of the lesson with studies, writers and concepts, for example.

Question at the end of the lesson: Plenaries summarise and pull together lessons. They offer a structure that students like and become familiar with.

Test your students regularly: One of the best ways for your students to remember what they've studied is to regularly test them. This ensures that there is no final push for revision based solely on remembering key terms or names.

Use Access to Scripts Service (see: http://www.aqa.org. uk/admin/p_results_access.php for details on how to do this): Instead of just learning through studying, students are better served going through pupil responses done under examination conditions. Depersonalise scripts, and then mark the scripts together explaining exactly what is needed for the highest marks. The best way to ensure a diversity of response is to ask for an A, C and E grade for any assessment window and module. These also act as an exemplar and assessment template for the teacher.

Other good techniques for success are revision sessions just before the examination. Take a simple breakfast, use revision games and go through past papers. All evidence shows this is a highly effective method of improving exam performance, especially if you can revise where the examination is due to take place. Evidence shows that people are likely to remember more in familiar surroundings.

The following tables set out the entire AS specification. It shows you where to locate the information in the student book and where to find the relevant lesson plans in the teacher's guide.

Unit One SCLY1: Culture and identity

Specification	Student book	Teacher's guide
Different types of culture	What is culture and identity?	Introduction to sociology Different conceptions of culture
Socialization	Socialization and the role of agencies	The socialization process and the agencies of socialization
Identity	Self, identity and difference	Functionalism and culture and identity Marxism and culture and identity Social action theory
Culture and age, disability, ethnicity, gender, nationality, sexuality and social class	The relationship of identity to different social groups	The relationship of identity to gender in contemporary society The relationship of identity to ethnicity in contemporary society The relationship of identity to social class in contemporary society Nationality Age Disability and sexuality
Leisure and identity	Leisure, consumption and identity	Leisure, consumption and identity

Unit One SCLY1: Families and households

Specification	Student book	Teacher's guide
How capitalism and social policies affect the family	The family in contemporary society	Introduction The relationship of the family to the social structure and the economy
How marriage is changing in contemporary society	The extent of family diversity	Changing patterns of marriage, cohabitation, separation, divorce, child-bearing and the life-course The diversity of contemporary family and household structures
The nature and extent of changes within the family	Domestic labour and gender roles in the family	Gender roles, domestic labour and power in the family
The sociology of childhood	Childhood	The nature of childhood and changes in the status of children
Population Trends in the family since 1900	Demographic trends since 1900	Demographic trends in the UK since 1900

Unit One SCLY1: Wealth, poverty and welfare

Specification	Student book	Teacher's guide
Definitions of wealth, poverty and welfare	Defining and measuring poverty, wealth and income	Different definitions and ways of measuring wealth, poverty and welfare
The location of poverty between different social groups	Poverty among different social groups	The distribution of poverty, wealth and income between different social groups
Why poverty endures within the UK	Sociological explanations of poverty	The existence and persistence of poverty in contemporary society
How social policy has been used to tackle poverty since 1940	Solutions to poverty and the role of social policy	Different responses to poverty, with particular reference to the role of social policy since the 1940s
How different organisations tackle poverty in the UK	Welfare pluralism	The nature and the role of the public, private, voluntary and informal welfare provision in contemporary society

The following table shows the breakdown of the specification for Unit Two, where the information can be found in the teacher book, the student book and the CD-ROM.

Unit Two SCLY2: Education

Specification	Student book	Teacher's guide
The role and purpose of education	Sociological views on education	An introduction to the role and purpose of education The role and purpose of education, including vocational education and training in contemporary society The role and purpose of education, including vocational education and training in contemporary society: Marxism The role and purpose of education
What happens within schools?	Relationships and processes within schools	Relationships and processes in schools
Different attainment by social group	Educational achievement and different social groups	Differential educational achievement by social groups Differential educational achievement by social groups by social class, gender and ethnicity
Polices and their importance	Educational policies	Educational policies
Applying research methods to the study of education	The application of research methods to education	The application of sociological research methods to the study of education

Topic Two SCLY2: Health and illness

Specification	Student book	Teacher's guide
The social construction of health, illness and disability	Health, illness and the body	Health, illness, disability and the body as social and biological constructs
How health and illness varies between social groups	The social distribution of health and illness by social groups	The unequal social distribution of health and illness by social groups
How provision varies between social groups	Health inequalities	Inequalities in health care
The sociology of mental illness	Mental illness	The sociological study of mental illness Mental interactionism and stigma
The role of doctors and care professionals	Medicine and health professionals	The role of health professionals
The use of research methods to study health	The application of research methods to health	Integrating theory and methods

Topic Two SCLY2: Sociological methods

Specification	Student book	Teacher's guide
An evaluation of quantitative and qualitative methods of research	Quantitative and qualitative methods and research design	Quantitative and qualitative methods of research
Different sources of data	Sources of data; their strengths and limitations	Sources of data and their strengths and limitations
The difference between primary and secondary data	Primary and secondary data	Sources of data and their strengths and limitations
The relationship between theory and methods	Positivism and interpretivism	The relationship between positivism, anti-positivism (interpretivism) and sociological methods
Theoretical and ethical and practical considerations	Theoretical, practical and ethical considerations	Theoretical, practical and ethical considerations Durkheim's study of suicide: bringing it all together

Schemes of work

The rest of this chapter sets out the suggested schemes of work for all sections, and include a summary of the teaching and learning activities outlines in the lesson plans.

SCLY1 Topic One: suggested scheme of work for *culture and identity*		
Week	**Specification content and objectives**	**Teacher learning and assessment activities**
1	Ice-breaker.	Draw society exercise. Cultural iceberg activity.
2	Different conceptions of culture including sub-culture, mass culture, high and low culture, popular culture and global culture.	Look at different cultures apart from our own. For example, how the Ashanti organise their family structures. Examine cases where no socialization process has occurred at all. A good example of this includes feral children and Genie. Produce a collage of high and low art images. Draw up a semi-structured questionnaire to carry out as homework to examine British culture and socialization.
3–5	The socialization process and the role of agencies of socialization.	Produce a pen pick of people on cards from different backgrounds from prompts from teacher. For example, person from middle/upper classes, public school educated, etc. List agencies that affect their personal identity. Ask them to divide the agencies into formal and informal. Group work involving research on different agencies of socialization. Produce a list of 'who am I' comments for the start of second lesson. Think how students' identities are influenced by other agencies. For example, their own peer group. Introduce functionalism, Marxism and social action theory. Use handouts describing theories, used as a basis for exercises. Mix and match to different theories and writers. Mix and match strengths and weaknesses to concepts. Produce a set of images that depict the theory given. Introduce images that have a number of interpretations. Use eye teasers that some can see and others cannot. Coverage of labelling and self-fulfilling prophecy.
5–8	The relationship of identity to age, disability, ethnicity, gender, nationality, sexuality and social class in contemporary society.	Introduce each section with images of various ways that each of the groups is seen. Define terms, such as 'sex', 'gender', 'nationality', etc. For each topic use videos to introduce changes that are occurring. Define the difference between 'sex' and 'gender', and relevant legislation such as the Equal Pay Act and the Sex Discrimination Act. Explain the difference between 'ethnicity' and 'race'. Discuss the distribution of wealth in the UK. Discuss how nationalism affects identity, with specific reference to the role of the mass media. Discuss article on homophobic bullying: http://www.bbc.co.uk/surgery/your_world/bullying/homophobia/. Cover the Civil Partnership Act and discussion on how homophobic bullying can affect a person's identity. Research on the Disability Discrimination Act.
9–10	Leisure, consumption and identity.	Use an image of a soap opera actor to introduce postmodernism. Produce timeline of premodernity, modernity and postmodernity. Compare postmodernist and Marxist views on leisure and identity.

SCLY1 Topic Two: suggested scheme of work for *family and households*		
Week	**Specification content and objectives**	**Teacher learning and assessment activities**
1–3	The relationship of the family to social structure and social change, with particular reference to the economy and state policies.	Starter: what does the family mean to you? Awareness that some issues may be sensitive needs to be included in any approach which involves examining a student's background. Support may be required in the classroom to ensure that no one is made to feel judged or excluded. Cover different family types: single parent, nuclear family, gay couple, matrifocal family, etc. Integrate theory and methods: students to interview those in different family types and write a report outlining what they have found. Investigate different forms of family structure from across the world: polygamy, polyandry, matrifocal family. Isolate advantages and disadvantages. Produce a timeline looking at preindustrial, industrial and postindustrial family structures. Introduce functionalist and New Right perspectives of the family. Produce a mobile, showing images of key writers, concepts, strengths and weaknesses, etc. Introduce Marxist and feminist views of the family. Starter: Marxist/feminist quotes. Lists of strengths and weaknesses activity. Cover key policies: SureStart, tax credits, maternity leave, etc.
2–4	Changing patterns of marriage, cohabitation, separation, divorce and child-bearing and the life-course, and the diversity of contemporary family and household structures.	Discuss issues with students: Do they plan to marry? Who is the major wage earner in their family? Who has the power in their family? Is the family nuclear or reconstituted? Who is the major carer? Are their parents cohabiting? Link these trends to family types. What is happening to family composition? How does this vary between ethnic groups? How many children are there in the average family? How many people are living alone? Why? What is happening to marriage rates? Divorces? Where are people marrying? Discuss age gaps between spouses, cohabitation, stepfamilies, completed family size, fertility rates, average age of first and second child, etc., births outside marriage, multiple births, teenage pregnancy, abortions and adoptions. The best way to achieve this is to split up tasks and ask the students to produce reports on each area. Download a copy of latest Social Trends file: http://www.statistics.gov.uk/downloads/theme_social/Social_Trends37/Social_Trends_37.pdf. This information could easily be found out by using a questionnaire. Ask the students to formulate questions that would elicit responses they require. Look at reasons for these trends. What reasons can they give for the trends they have isolated? What are the consequences of these trends? For example, divorce rates impact on cohabitation rates, and so on. Presentations on students' findings. Discuss sociological explanations of divorce. Introduce key studies on family diversity, such as Rapoport's categories of diversity and Eversley and Bonnerjea's work on regional and geographical diversity. Contrast these to sociologists who believe diversity is limited (such as Chester's work on the neo-conventional family). Discuss sociological views on one-parent families.

3–6	The nature and extent of changes within the family, with reference to gender roles, domestic labour and power relationships.	Introduce the concept of conjugal roles using the historical context of Willmott and Young's study.
		Students could look at a range of studies that examine conjugal roles. For example, the impact of employment on symmetry, income and education (Man-Yee-Kan), age, the role of grandparents, dual burden and emotional participation (Dunscombe and Marsden).
		Design a questionnaire on household tasks in the students' families. Look at areas such as who buys shoes and school clothes, knowing the children's likes and dislikes, sorting out problems at school, and so on.
		Discuss the problems of such studies. How do we define housework for example? How valid are methods that collate such data? Can we be sure that diaries are accurate?
		Look at power relationships. Complete a questionnaire on power in the family. This can be done by replicating Edgell's study, *Middle Class Couples* (1980). Also have a look at Pahl's work (1993) in terms of financial arrangements.
		Discuss the preparation of food in the family. Who gets the largest portion? Who is served first? Who gets the choicest cuts?
		Remember that sometimes decision making is more complex than the above, with some partners not having the power to prevent others from making decisions, whilst agenda setting is also important. Why do we assume that women are most appropriate for the expressive role?
		Discuss the dark side of the family.
6–8	The nature of childhood and changes in the status of children in the family and society.	Explain cultural and biological indicators of childhood.
		Construct a quiz on the different ages a person can start to do things in the UK. For example, the following website can be used to assist: http://www.connexions-somerset.org.uk/rights/areyouoldenough.html. Think about how different age groups would behave; their politics, interests, income, transport, outlook, etc.
		Produce a timeline starting from 1780 going up to the present day. Add the following on the timeline: social attitudes towards children, their dress, whether at school or not, social policies introduced (for example, the Forster Act 1870), employment legislation and any social problems associated with children.
		List ways in which society has become 'child centred'. How do we protect our children? What books do we consult? How do we treat children in a special way? For example, clothes, food and holidays.
		Postman's views on the 'death of childhood'.
9–10	Demographic trends in the UK since 1900; Reasons for changes in birth rates, death rates and family size.	Research task on average life expectancies.
		Activity: Reasons for increases/decreases in birth rates, death rates and family size.
		Analyse census.

SCLY1 Topic Three: suggested scheme of work for *wealth, poverty and welfare*		
Week	**Specification content and objectives**	**Teacher learning and assessment activities**
1–2	Different definitions and ways of measuring poverty, wealth and income.	Define terminology. What do we mean by wealth, income and poverty? Give examples. Card sort activity to cover different definitions of poverty. Coverage of key studies that have aimed to measure poverty. Activity: Poverty and Social Exclusion Survey list: http://www.jrf.org.uk/knowledge/findings/socialpolicy/930.asp. Define wealth. Discuss the problems of defining and measuring wealth and poverty. Guess the wealth of celebrities activity at: http://business.timesonline.co.uk/tol/business/specials/rich_list/rich_list_search/. Presentations on world poverty.
3–5	The distribution of poverty, wealth and income between different social groups.	Distribute Inland Revenue statistics: http://www.hmrc.gov.uk/stats/personal_wealth/table13_5.pdf. What do the students notice? Has inequality increased or decreased? Why do they think this might be the case? List the groups that students think are poor in the UK. Why are they so at risk? Group exercise to look at poverty. Which areas are poorest? Why? Which social groups? Research activity on how class is measured in the UK. (To see the eight official social classes in the UK, use: http://www.statistics.gov.uk/methods_quality/ns_sec/cat_desc_op_issue.asp).
5–7	The existence and persistence of poverty in contemporary society.	Write down five reasons why students think poverty continues to be a major issue in contemporary society. Link to right and left wing views of poverty. Coverage of Murray's controversial study on the 'underclass' (see: www.civitas.org.uk/pdf/cw33.pdf and www.civitas.org.uk/pdf/cs10.pdf), Interview people about poverty. Do they blame the individual? Or society? Cover the social democratic view of poverty. Research task on the key benefits available and the current rates of the national minimum wage. Key concept cards for Marxism activity.
8–10	Different responses to poverty, with particular reference to the role of social policy since 1940.	Ask students to come up with their own ideas about how to solve poverty. Reintroduce the ideas of the New Right, social democratic solutions, Marxist solutions and feminist solutions. How would each want to solve the issues of poverty? Research their solutions. What are the advantages of these and what are the disadvantages? Create timeline of the welfare state since 1940.
11–12	The nature and role of public, private, voluntary and informal welfare provision in contemporary society.	Activity: Matching definitions. Think about how present welfare provision is made. Produce a timeline of major welfare acts with images, etc. Mix and match examples of voluntary, private and public welfare provision. Look at examples of informal provision of welfare. What are the advantages and disadvantage of this approach? Debate: Means-tested benefits.

SCLY2 Topic Four: suggested scheme of work for *education*		
Week	**Specification content and objectives**	**Teacher learning and assessment activities**
1–4	The role and purpose of education, including vocational education and training, in contemporary society.	Conduct student interviews to record the education history of each student. Introduce functionalism and the work of Parsons, Durkheim and Davis and Moore through a concept wall activity. An introduction to Marxism and the work of Willis and Bowles and Gintis through a concept wall activity and 'mix and match' card sort. Discuss the 'ideal pupil' and the hidden curriculum. Starter: Vocational course acronyms. Research using prospectuses. Class debate on vocational education.
5–7	Relationships and processes within schools, with particular reference to teacher/ pupil relationships, pupil sub-cultures, the hidden curriculum, and the organisation of teaching and learning.	Starter activity: 'Guess the attributes' to introduce labelling. Activity: 'Jumbled up' self-fulfilling prophecy. Cover key interactionist studies (Becker, Rosenthal and Jacobsen, Connolly). Create mind maps. Discuss different youth groups and behaviour at school. Cover studies on sub-cultures, including revision of Willis. Research tasks and group presentations.
8–12	Differential educational achievement of social groups by social class, gender and ethnicity in contemporary society.	Starter activity: Hangman. Analyse league tables. Complete table containing theories of working class underachievement (coverage of Bernstein, Bourdieu, Rist, etc.). Analysis of GCSE and A level results by gender. Cover classic studies showing patriarchy in education (Sharpe, Spender, Stanworth and Kelly). Observe a science lesson. Cover theories on why girls outperform boys. Activity: 'Jumbled up' A grade essay. Analyse GCSE and A level results by ethnic group. Research activity: theories of underachievement of ethnic minorities. Content analysis of textbooks to check for racism/ethnocentricity.
13–14	The significance of educational policies, including selection, comprehensivisation and marketisation, for an understanding of the structure, role, impact and experience of education.	Starter activity: Life in 1860. Cover 1870 and 1944 acts. Read out eleven-plus test questions and ask students to answer them in timed conditions (see: www.elevenplusexams.co.uk/). Analyse the effects of these acts on different social groups. Card sort activity where students match key components of the 1988 act (Ofsted, national curriculum, SATS, league tables, CTCs, etc.) with the correct descriptions. Gap-fill exercise at: http://www.educationforum.co.uk/sociology_2/historyeducation.htm. Debate: EMA. Compile list of different types of secondary schools today. Cover Curriculum 200 and new specialised diplomas. Discuss how much university will cost.

| 14–18 | The application of sociological research methods to the study of education. | Starter activity: 'Find a study'.
Group research activity on strengths and weaknesses of a specific qualitative research method in educational research.
Use a research method in school.
Card sort activity: Match sociologist to method.
Group research activity on strengths and weaknesses of a specific quantitative method in educational research.
Activity: Primary and secondary data 'post it on the board'.
Discuss Marxist and interactionist views on league tables.
Discuss the value of public documents: your school's Ofsted report.
Cover Hey's study and the usefulness of life documents. |

SCLY2 Topic Five: suggested scheme of work for *health*

Week	Specification content and objectives	Teacher learning and assessment activities
1–2	Health, illness, disability and the body as social and biological constructs.	Compare student definitions of health to the World Health Organisation (WHO), (http://www.who.int/about/definition/en/print.html). Cover health and illness as social constructs. Compare student definitions of disability to the Disability Discrimination Act definition. Research the biomedical and social models of health, share ideas between groups. Discuss what the 'perfect' male and female bodies are. Cover the body as a social construct. Create a timeline showing major medical advances (link to medical model) and rise of complementary medicine (link to social model). Research activity involving the medicalisation of different conditions, pregnancy, disability, etc.
3–6	The unequal social distribution of health and illness in the United Kingdom by social class, age, gender, ethnicity, region and internationally.	Investigate ways of defining social class. Research activity on links between social class and health (http://www.statistics.gov.uk/ssd/surveys/general_household_survey.asp). Discuss the Black Report (www.scotpho.org.uk/nmsruntime/saveasdialog.asp?lID = 1057&sID = 1655). Discuss health inequalities (Shaw, Smith and Dorling: http://www.bmj.com/cgi/content/full/330/7498/1016). Cover the two main explanations of why the working classes are most likely to suffer from poor health (cultural and structural). Compare with other explanations such as the artefact approach and the theory of social selection. Starter activity: 'True or false' gender facts. Analyse *General Household Survey* on gender and health. Cover theories that explain gender differences in health. Card sort activity. Questionnaire on gender and health. Analyse patterns of morbidity and mortality for different ethnic groups (http://www.raceequalityfoundation.org.uk/hsc/files/health-brief6.pdf). Complete table showing description and evaluation of each theory on ethnicity and health. Starter activity: Mock 'postcode lottery'. Discuss article on inverse care law (http://www.guardian.co.uk/society/2000/nov/09/NHS).
7	Inequalities in the provision of, and access to, health care in contemporary society.	Create a timeline to show key changes in NHS provision and services. Create mind maps to show how access to health varies by social group. Poster creation activity comparing NHS to private health care.

8–10	The sociological study of the nature and social distribution of mental illness.	Activity: List of 'normal' and 'abnormal' behaviours. Activity: defining key terms. Cover the history of mental illness. Discuss exorcism article (http://www.guardian.co.uk/society/2001/may/02/socialcare.mentalhealth1). Cover the social groups most affected by mental illness. Starter activity: The religious man. Cover labelling and self-fulfilling prophecy, and how this applied to mental health. Analyse key studies (Rosenhan, Goffman and Foucault). Class debate: Interactionists versus Realists. Student research activity on specific mental disorders and their portrayal by the media.
11	The role of medicine and the health professions.	Team game: 'Back to the board'. Worksheets on how different perspectives view medicine and health professionals. Cover the professionalization of nursing. Research and discuss tasks and pay of different doctors.
12	The application of sociological research methods to the study of health.	Card sort activity: Matching sociologists to research studies. Individual tasks, researching one sociological method from spec and analysing its usefulness in health research. Student production of report and handout of chosen method.

SCLY2 Topic Six: suggested scheme of work for *sociological methods*		
Week	**Specification content and objectives**	**Teacher learning and assessment activities**
1–3	Quantitative and qualitative methods of research; their strengths and limitations; research design.	Starter activity: 'Imagine you are a sociologist'. Cover new terms such as 'subjectivity', 'objectivity', 'qualitative', 'quantitative', 'correlation', 'generalisation', 'empirical', 'validity' and 'reliability'. Activity: 'What am I?' Textbook research: Find explanations of the main research methods. Hypotheses activity. Mini raffle to demonstrate sampling. Cover sampling frames and main sampling methods. Create questionnaires to show the importance of pilot studies.
4–9	Sources of data, including questionnaires, interviews, participant and non-participant observation, experiments, documents, and official statistics; the strengths and limitations of these sources.	Define 'experiment'. Activity: Match cards on the board. Use textbooks and notes from previous modules to find studies involving experiments. Create tables to assess strengths and weaknesses of experiments and questionnaires. Create spider diagram to show how questionnaire response rates can be improved. Print this web page out and ask the students to think up some disadvantages of longitudinal surveys: http://news.bbc.co.uk/1/hi/education/705793.stm. Analyse types of studies using: http://www.socialresearchmethods.net/tutorial/Cho2/cho1.html. Group research project on a specific longitudinal study using: http://www.iser.essex.ac.uk/ulsc/about/whatlong.php. Discuss how to answer exam style question. An account of 'what happened last lesson' to introduce observation. Read and discuss extracts from key studies. Conduct interviews to explain 'interviewer bias'. Complete the census form: http://www.statistics.gov.uk/census2001/censusform.asp. List major government reports and types of official statistics. Starter activity: 'Find a card then find a partner'. Presentations using overhead projector on a specific secondary source. Cover John Scott's criteria.

		The distinction between primary and secondary data, and between quantitative and qualitative data.	Covered within lessons 1–9.
10		The relationship between positivism, interpretivism and sociological methods; the nature of 'social facts'.	Discuss 'What is science?' and cover Giddens' definition. Discuss whether sociology meets the criteria of science. Revise positivism and interpretivism. Activity: University prospectuses: Is sociology a BA or a BSc?
11–12		The theoretical, practical and ethical considerations influencing choice of topic, choice of method(s) and the conduct of research.	Define practical, theoretical and ethical considerations. Discus the importance of each of these. Analyse key studies (Laud Humphreys, *The Tearoom Trade* [1970]; James Patrick, *A Glasgow Gang Observed* [1973]; Rosenthal and Jacobsen's *Pygmalion in the Classroom* [1968]; Dunning et al., *The Roots of Football Hooliganism*; and finally Eileen Barker, *Making of a Moonie* [1984]) to decide on whether the sociologist was influenced by practical, theoretical or ethical considerations. Create posters showing ethical conduct for sociologists. Analyse Durkheim's study on suicide to draw whole module together.

Topic 1

Culture and identity

Lesson One: Introduction to sociology

Topic	Group	Ability	No. of boys	No. of girls	No. of special educational needs' students (SEN)	Teaching assistant
Ice-breaker lesson: Introducing sociology.		AS/A2				

Start positive	Introduce the students to the sociology course. A number of starters are useful. For example, ask them to name their favourite animal.
Connect learning	Ask the students what sociology is; write the responses on the whiteboard.
Share learning objectives	• Bond the group/act as an ice-breaker. • Set expectations for the course. • Explain assessment objectives. • Formulate what the students would like to study. • Give a sociological journal to each of the students and encourage them to use it to insert articles from quality daily newspapers such as the *Guardian*, the *Times*, and so on.
Lesson outline	Looking at the course in general and thinking about British culture.
Starter hook	Ask the students to work in pairs and introduce their partners to the rest of the group.
Activity One	Give each student a blank piece of A3 paper. Ask them to draw a picture of what they think British society looks like. Assure them that you are not interested in the quality of their drawings, but the ideas. Give them 15 minutes, allowing them to colour etc.
Activity Two	Ask each student to explain to the group what they have drawn and their reasons.
Activity Three	Give out pro forma that you have already prepared that explains what the different shapes mean.
Review learning	• What is sociology? • What does society look like? • How many modules do you sit for AS? • What is your sociological journal to be used for?
Preview next lesson	Looking at different cultures.
End positively	Tell the students it was an excellent lesson. Thank them for their contributions.
What the examiners are looking for	Examiners want to see that students have a good contemporary knowledge of British society. One area that examiners like to see is students using diagrams to explain concepts. So when they are explaining Marxism, encourage them to draw a pyramid to contextualise it in the examination or in an essay answer.
Homework	Ask the students to cut out and analyse two articles about 'British culture' from a quality newspaper and analyse the content.
Getting the most out of your class	A good ice-breaker exercise offers an excellent chance for you to differentiate in terms of ability. Ask more detailed questions about their drawings. Provide homework that allows extension for the most able students.

Lesson Two: Different conceptions of culture

Topic	Group	Ability	No. of boys	No. of girls	No. of SEN	Teaching assistant
Introduction to sociology.		AS/A2				

Start positive	Tell the students they had an excellent start to their AS course last lesson and that good contributions were made.
Connect learning	<ul><li>What is sociology?</li><li>What is assessed in AO1 and AO2?</li><li>Tell the class about something currently in the news that has interested you.</li></ul>
Share learning objectives	<ul><li>For students to be able to define culture.</li><li>Appreciate cultural diversity.</li><li>The importance of the socialisation process.</li><li>Be aware that sub-cultures exist, even in cohesive societies.</li></ul>
Lesson outline	Playing the iceberg game (see *starter hook*), followed by a case study of non-socialised citizens.
Starter hook	Draw an iceberg on the whiteboard or use an overlay. Ask the students to write obvious words relating to British culture on the visible area of the iceberg and the hidden, undesirable or ignored aspects of British culture on the area below the waterline. For example, one obvious aspect of British culture is 'tea': this would go onto the visible part of the iceberg. An example of the 'dark side' of British culture is 'binge drinking': this would therefore go below the waterline.
Activity One	Introduce a case study where socialization has failed to occur. This links nicely to AS level Psychology and the idea of deprivation. It might be appropriate to use Curtis's Genie example from Los Angeles, or Kamala and Amala from India. Compare what these girls and Genie could do compared to a child aged six in our own culture.
Activity Two	Produce a set of cards containing words such as 'values', 'norms', 'mores', 'customs', 'culture', 'mass culture', 'popular culture', 'global culture', 'biology', 'secondary socialization', 'primary socialization' and 'deviance'. On separate cards prepare definitions of each of the words. Ask the students to match up the words with the correct definitions.
Activity Three	Introduce the idea of high and low culture. Ask the students to produce a mobile or collage of either high or low cultural images. Ask them to explain to the rest of the class why they have chosen each image.
Review learning	<ul><li>What are 'norms', 'values', 'culture', 'customs', 'socialization', etc?</li><li>How important is socialization?</li><li>What happens to language and behaviour when they are not taught?</li><li>Give an example of high culture.</li><li>Give an example of low culture.</li></ul>
Preview next lesson	Looking at the socialization process.
End positively	Tell the students it was an excellent lesson, particularly the contribution from X about Y.
What the examiners are looking for	Sociology revolves around the use of appropriate terminology and vocabulary. When using this kind of language students gain AO2 marks if they can contextualise such terminology.
Homework	Learn the definitions to the key words learned today, either by creating a 'sociology glossary' or by creating a 'key terms' poster.
Getting the most from your class	For differentiation (allowing for different levels of difficulty by outcome), ask students to rank key words in order of importance. Give appropriate examples of each. As always, use questioning at the end of the lesson to identify whether learning has occurred.

Lesson 3

Lesson Three: The socialization process and the agencies of socialization

Topic	Group	Ability	No. of boys	No. of girls	No. of SEN	Teaching assistant
The socialization process.		AS/A2				

Connect learning	• What are 'norms', 'values', 'culture', 'primary socialization' and 'secondary socialization'? • What happens if socialization does not occur? Give an example. • Give examples of some aspects of British culture that are overt and some that are less obvious.
Share learning objectives	• Understand the importance of socialization. • Explore the factors that impact on our social identity. • Understand appropriate terminology and be able to use it in context. • Introduce concepts of formal and informal social control.
Lesson outline	Exploring culture and socialization in modern contemporary Britain.
Starter hook	Show the students an image of a person; someone they don't know. Ask them to produce their ideas of what the person's hobbies, likes, dislikes, and so on are. Explore the impact of social influences as opposed to biological differences. Images might include a public schoolchild, a criminal, a single female and a working-class person.
Activity One	Ask students to list agencies that affect their personal identity (students will need the concept of 'agency' explained first). The best way to do this is to ask the students to list them in chronological order from birth to death. These could be captured on the whiteboard for students to note down. Then explain the difference between formal and informal social control. Ask the students to divide the agencies on the whiteboard into formal and informal.
Activity Two	Ask the students what they have eaten in the last 24 hours. Ask them to produce a spider diagram: what they ate, where they got the food from, what companies were involved in the food production, the countries the food was originally from, and so on. Key concepts such as globalisation should be explained and captured on whiteboard.
Activity Three	Ask the students to form four groups. Give each group the task of researching in more detail how one agency affects our socialization (agencies covered should include family, education, mass media, and religion). Have a range of textbooks available for this activity. Each group could produce a handout summarising their findings, which can then be photocopied for all students.
Review learning	• Provide some agencies that affect socialization. • Ask the students to explain which are the most important of these agencies.
Preview next lesson	Looking at perspectives on culture and identity.
End positively	Tell the students it was another good lesson looking at socialization.
What the examiners are looking for	Examiners like to see that students can spell terminology, so when you test your students give half marks for misspelling either a concept or a key writer.
Homework	Ask the students to do a mini project on factors that affect our identity.
Getting the most out of your class	One way to improve students' terminology is for them to construct a glossary. Alternatively why not regularly test students to see if they understand and remember the terms they are covering?

Lesson Four: Functionalism and culture and identity

Topic	Group	Ability	No. of boys	No. of girls	No. of SEN	Teaching assistant
Perspectives on culture and identity.		AS/A2				

Start positive	Tell the students it was an excellent lesson on key words and British culture last time.
Connect learning	• Give an example of a social difference • Give an example of a biological difference • What does 'quantitative' mean? • What does 'qualitative' mean?
Share learning objectives	• Know key word terminology for functionalism. • Link functionalism with appropriate key writers. • Understand the strengths and weaknesses of functionalism. • Relate functionalism to the production of culture.
Lesson outline	Introducing functionalist key ideas and writers and to evaluate the theory.
Starter hook	Ask your students to produce a list of ideas about who they are.
Activity One	Go through key concepts for functionalists including 'structuralism', 'norms', 'values', 'value consensus', 'functional prerequisites' and 'role allocation'. Explain key writers, staring off with Durkheim and social solidarity. Ask the students if there is social solidarity in modern Britain. List factors that suggest harmony and those that suggest otherwise. Try to ensure that the focus is on culture. So, for example, discuss what the features are that ensure social solidarity, collective consciousness, common experiences, common norms and values.
Activity Two	A good way to introduce concepts such as functionalism is to have concept walls in the classroom. Provide card, felt-tip pens, magazines, and so on, and ask the students to produce a card for each key concept, writer, and strengths and weaknesses of functionalism. Ask the students place images of Durkheim, Parsons, Davis and Moore on their concept walls.
Activity Three	To end key concept lessons it is very useful to explain the importance of evaluation. One way to introduce this is to place strengths and weaknesses of functionalism into a card sort. Ask the students to sort them into advantages and disadvantages. Then ask them to take turns explaining them to the rest of the group.
Review learning	• Why is functionalism so named? • Name the key writers associated with functionalism. • Give a strength of functionalism. • Give a weakness of functionalism. • Why is 'structural theory' so named?
Preview next lesson	Exploring Marxism.
End positively	Tell the students it was an excellent lesson looking at functionalism and culture.
What the examiners are looking for	Examiners like to see students using their tool kit of different theories. Given that these theories overlap across the course it is vital to introduce and test them at this early stage. Names and concepts need to be learned; however, dates are not quite so important.
Homework	Ask the students to write three paragraphs explaining what functionalism is and how functionalists explain culture and identity.
Getting the most out of your class	An excellent way to introduce concepts is to produce a concept wall for all theories. This allows you to continually test and remind students about key theories. It also allows you to brighten up your classroom with displays that reinforce daily learning.

Lesson Five: Marxism and culture and identity

Topic	Group	Ability	No. of boys	No. of girls	No. of SEN	Teaching assistant
Perpsectives on culture and identity.		AS/A2				

Start positive	Tell the students it was a good lesson on functionalism last time and recap on what they learned.
Connect learning	• Why is functionalism so named? • How is culture internalised according to functionalism? • Name a key writer associated with the theory. • Give one strength and one weakness of the theory.
Share learning objectives	• Know key word terminology for Marxism. • Link Marxism with the appropriate key writers. • Understand the strengths and weaknesses of Marxism. • Relate culture to Marxism.
Lesson outline	Introducing key concepts of Marxism and relating them to culture and identity.
Starter hook	Ask the students to in turn write a key word, concept, writer, or strength or criticism on the whiteboard (or graffiti board). Once complete use a digital camera to take a photo of the whiteboard and give a copy to the students.
Activity One	Introduce and explain concepts including 'bourgeoisie', 'proletariat', 'superstructure', 'infrastructure', 'false consciousness', 'surplus value', 'class consciousness' and 'means of production'. Reinforce learning by way of a handout of the concepts. Mix and match key concepts together, either with a card sort, or word mix and match. Link the notion of false consciousness to the notion of identity: the proletariat do not realise the true nature of their exploitation and thus could be said to have a false sense of identity.
Activity Two	A good way to introduce concepts such as Marxism is to have concept walls in the classroom. Provide card, felt-tips pens, magazines, and so on, and ask the students to produce a card for each key concept, writer, and strengths and weaknesses of Marxism. Ask the students place images of Marx, Engels and other key writers onto the wall.
Activity Three	Try using images to link to concepts. This can be a good group exercise. Compare a selection of images from a sports page to explain false consciousness, an image of the Russian revolution, and so on.
Review learning	• What is the infrastructure? • What is the superstructure? • Who are the bourgeoisie? • Who are the proletariat? • What is false consciousness?
Preview next lesson	Exploring social action theory.
End positively	Tell the students it was a good lesson examining the difficult concept of Marxism.
What the examiners are looking for	Examiners want to see a real understanding of concepts such as Marxism. Ensure that you relate them to modern society. Which states, for example, can be said to be still Marxist in orientation? Who leads these states? Where are they located?
Homework	Ask the students to work out strengths and weaknesses of Marxism using the following exercise to encourage the students to use the skills of evaluation. Type out a number of advantages and disadvantages, then ask the students to isolate each of them in turn.
Getting the most out of your class	For extension activities ask the students to find images of Marx, Engels, Trotsky and Louis Althusser. (For appropriate images of key sociologists direct them to: http://www.marxists.org/archive/marx/photo/index.htm).

Lesson Six: Social action theory

Topic	Group	Ability	No. of boys	No. of girls	No. of SEN	Teaching assistant
Sources and conceptions of the self, identity and difference.		AS/A2				

Start positive	Tell the students it was a good lesson on Marxism last time. Recap what they produced.
Connect learning	• Who are the bourgeoisie? • What do the bourgeoisie own? • Who are the proletariat? • Who creates culture?
Share learning objectives	• Know key word terminology for social action theory. • Link social action theory with appropriate key writers. • Understand the strengths and weaknesses of social action theory.
Lesson outline	Explore the key writers of social action theory.
Starter hook	Show the students the following optical illusion and ask them what they see: http://www.qualitytrading.com/illusions/girlwoman.html.
Activity One	Show an image of a soldier in a war-torn area with children around the soldier. Ask the students to come up with speech bubbles for the soldier and the children. They should come up with many different interpretations. Explain what the onlookers might be thinking.
Activity Two	Give the students a handout detailing the work of Weber and his views on verstehen, then focus on Becker or another prominent theorist to introduce the concept of labelling and self-fulfilling prophecy. The key point to get across is that an individual's sense of self is affected by the opinions and reactions of others.
Activity Three	Ask the students to work out the differences between sentences that explain the macro approach to sociology and contrast these with some micro statements. Ask the students to summarise the differences.
Review learning	• Name a writer associated with social action theory. • What is verstehen? • What method would a social action theorist tend to use? • Explain self-fulfilling prophesy. • What is a 'master status'? • Who are the agents of social control?
Preview next lesson	Exploring identity and gender.
End positively	Tell the students it was a thought-provoking lesson on social class and culture.
What the examiners are looking for	Examiners are keen to ensure that students make the link between theory and methods. It is therefore vital that you encourage research using methods at an early stage. However, make sure the students know that in reality most sociologists use a combination of quantitative and qualitative methods.
Homework	Design a presentation explaining the social action explanation of self and identity. Include an evaluation, referring to Marxism and functionalism.
Getting the most out of your class	Create a concept wall. Add images or place strengths and weaknesses onto the wall. Or why not use a desktop publishing package and projector?

Lesson 7

Lesson Seven: The relationship of identity to gender in contemporary society

Topic	Group	Ability	No. of boys	No. of girls	No. of SEN	Teaching assistant
Identity and gender.		AS/A2				

Start positive	Tell the students it was a good lesson on social action theory last time.
Connect learning	• What is verstehen? • Explain the method that social action theorists would tend to use. • What is the self-fulfilling prophesy? • Give a criticism of the self-fulfilling prophesy. • Name another interactionist writer apart from Weber. • What is a master status?
Share learning objectives	• Understand the concepts of age, disability, ethnicity, nationality, sexuality and social class. • Relate these concepts to culture. • Be aware of strengths and weaknesses.
Lesson outline	An assessment of the relationship between gender and culture.
Starter hook	Give out a set of words – such as 'strong', 'intelligent', 'witty', and so on – printed on card and ask the students to decide whether they would ascribe each quality to males or females.
Activity One	Create a word sort. Ask the students to sort examples of biological differences from cultural differences. Are these ideas changing? Use a similar list of jobs and ask the students to isolate female and male jobs. Which are of higher status? Which are lower paid? Ask the students to make notes on the difference between sex and gender, and relevant legislation such as the Equal Pay Act and the Sex Discrimination Act.
Activity Two	At this point it is useful to introduce ideas from popular films. A good film to use is *The Full Monty* (1997). Show the students the scene where a woman uses a urinal in the male toilets. Ask the students to isolate where there is a 'crisis'. Ask them what evidence they can find to suggest that patriarchy is no longer as powerful as it once was.
Activity Three	Give the students a handout that covers the key ideas of feminism and the feminist views of culture and identity, followed by some theory on the crisis in masculinity.
Review learning	• What is sex? • What is gender? • Is there a crisis of masculinity? • What is the 'glass ceiling'? • What is content analysis?
Preview next lesson	Looking at identity and ethnicity.
End positively	Tell the students it was an excellent lesson exploring the concept of identity and gender.
What the examiners are looking for	Examiners are always surprised when students appear to believe that feminists are a single group. Encourage students to memorise the three types of feminism. Provide key words for each: 'L' word for liberal feminists (legislation), 'C' word for Marxist feminists (root cause of oppression is capitalism), and 'P' word for radical feminists (patriarchy, the male domination of society).
Homework	Ask the students to write a review of 'portrayals of men and women' from a lad's magazine such as *FHM* or *Loaded*, or do the same looking at women's magazines. Are gender roles still different? How are men becoming more like women and vice versa?
Getting the most out of your class	Encourage the students to have concept pages in a notebook. Regularly mark them and ask more able students to extend and refine their ideas and link them to contemporary British society.

Lesson Eight: The relationship of Identity to ethnicity in contemporary society

Topic	Group	Ability	No. of boys	No. of girls	No. of SEN	Teaching assistant
Identity and ethnicity.		AS/A2				

Start positive	Tell the students it was a good lesson on gender last time.
Connect learning	<ul><li>What is sex?</li><li>What is gender?</li><li>Is there a crisis of masculinity?</li><li>What is the 'glass ceiling'?</li></ul>
Share learning objectives	<ul><li>Understand the concepts of age, disability, ethnicity, nationality, sexuality and social class.</li><li>Relate the concepts to culture.</li><li>Understand strengths and weaknesses of the concepts.</li></ul>
Lesson outline	Focusing on ethnicity and culture and identity.
Starter hook	Ask the students to write down as many ethnic groups that they can think of that live in England and Wales.
Activity One	Explain the difference between ethnicity and race. Why could the term 'race' be seen as unacceptable by some sociologists? What characteristics do ethnic groups have? Ask students to note down their answers and then compare.
Activity Two	Construct a race quiz. Ask the students what they know about race and the UK. Ask them questions on how many languages are spoken, where Cliff Richard was born, crime rates and ethnicity, and so on. You could extend this activity by discussing the meaning and derivation of words such as 'ketchup' and 'jodhpur'. Give the students a handout, or research using textbooks, to learn how ethnicity shapes identity.
Activity Three	Using Taylor's *Investigating Culture and Identity* (1997) on cultural hybrids, ask the students to come up with a list of examples from their own experience. Use the first 10 minutes of the film *East is East* (1999) to illustrate the concept.
Review learning	<ul><li>What is racism?</li><li>Explain the term 'stereotyping'.</li><li>Give some indication of racism in the UK.</li><li>Give an example of hybrid identities.</li><li>What is institutional racism?</li></ul>
Preview next lesson	Examining how social class is ascertained.
End positively	Tell the students it was an interesting lesson on social class and lifestyles.
What the examiners are looking for	Examiners want to read responses from students who are aware of the complexities of modern society. Encourage them to learn that Asian people come from an incredibly large geographical area. Have a map of the world in the classroom and use the Internet to show labelled images of different areas and people.
Homework	Ask the students to write an essay: Examine the ways in which gender and ethnicity can shape identity (approximately 300–500 words). By this stage students should be practising exam-style essays.
Getting the most out of your class	When doing project work think about which task is easiest. Divide students into two groups: those most likely to be working at grade C and below, and those above, in the order of most difficult task to easiest. Or mix and match individuals of various ability within the groups to ensure a wider breadth of experience.

Lesson Nine: The relationship of identity to social class in contemporary society

Topic	Group	Ability	No. of boys	No. of girls	No. of SEN	Teaching assistant
Identity and class.		AS/A2				

Start positive	Tell the students it was a good lesson on ethnicity last lesson.
Connect learning	• What is racism? • Explain the term 'stereotyping'. • Give some indication of racism in the UK. • Give an example of hybrid identities. • What is institutional racism?
Share learning objectives	• Understand how class background is ascertained. • The effect class has on identity in contemporary Britain.
Lesson outline	Focussing on how social class affects identity.
Starter hook	Produce a set of images of people from different class backgrounds. Ask the students to explain where they think the people in the images were educated, what their pastimes might be, their occupation, diet, clothes, voting behaviour, and so on. This could be produced by a cut-out with students adding their observations. Initiate a group discussion on 'what is social class'?
Activity One	Show the students clips from the film *Brassed Off* (1996) to show the idea of working-class culture. Ask the students if this culture is dying out and why this might this be the case. Ask them if we are becoming a country of middle-class people. Perhaps show them evidence of the declining readership of the tabloids and discuss. To contrast this view, show the students the *Times Rich List*. Initiate a discussion about the distribution of wealth in the UK: what does it tell us about the significance of social class today? Go to: http://business.timesonline.co.uk/tol/business/specials/rich_list/?CMP=KNC-IX7429721604&HBX_PK=times+rich+list&HBX_OU=50.
Activity Two	Discuss how class affects identity, asking the students to research this using the student book. Links should be made to Lesson Five: Marxism.
Activity Three	Ask the students to produce a questionnaire that finds out whether class is still important.
Review learning	• How is class measured? • What impact does class have on lifestyle? Give an indication of this difference. • Name and provide an explanation of a class group in modern Britain. • Name newspapers that would typically be read by the working classes, middle classes and upper classes.
Preview next lesson	Exploring the idea of nationalism.
End positively	Tell the students you're really pleased at how well they all remembered Marxism.
What the examiners are looking for	Class is one of the core themes in the new specification. It is thus vital that the students understand class, how it is worked out and the key terminology that is used.
Homework	Using the questionnaires the students created, ask the students to ask 10 people their views on social class.
Getting the most out of your class	Students can be made aware of how class influences all our life chances. Production of questionnaires also provides a chance for weaker students to gain confidence, whilst more able candidates can extend their knowledge and produce hypotheses that occur as a result of responses from the questionnaires.

Lesson Ten: Nationality

Topic	Group	Ability	No. of boys	No. of girls	No. of SEN	Teaching assistant
Identity and nationality.		AS/A2				

Start positive	Tell the students that it was a good lesson on social class and identity last time, especially the work on X by Y.
Connect learning	<ul><li>Name one scale used to measure social class.</li><li>What is social mobility?</li><li>How do our life chances change with our class background?</li><li>Name the sociological theory that views class as being fundamental.</li><li>Explain how class affects voting, press readership and education.</li></ul>
Share learning objectives	<ul><li>Understand nationalism.</li><li>How nation states are formed and the sub-divisions that result.</li><li>Contemporary issues surrounding nationalism in the UK; for example, the devolution and growth of the Scottish National Party (SNP) and the British National Party (BNP) are worth considering.</li></ul>
Lesson outline	An exploration of what nationality is and examples of nation states and the divisions that these cause.
Starter hook	Ask the students if they see themselves as nationalistic. Perhaps show them a clip of a British athlete or tennis player or the national football team scoring a goal to prompt them to discuss how it makes them feel.
Activity One	Ask the students to research some of the terminology related to nationalism. On the Internet ask them to look up 'nation', 'state', 'nationalism', 'patriotism', 'BNP' and 'Enoch Powell'. Ask them to discuss what is happening in the UK, what a Member of the Scottish Parliament (MSP) is and what devolution is.
Activity Two	Ask the students to explore and research how nationalism affects identity, with specific reference to the role of the mass media.
Activity Three	Students could use a questionnaire to measure just how patriotic people in the UK feel. How could you operationalise this concept? Ask the students to construct the questionnaire, use it and then report back their findings.
Review learning:	<ul><li>Give an example of a nation state.</li><li>Give an example of patriotism.</li><li>What is the problem with patriotism? Contextualise this problem; use Israel, for example.</li><li>What is devolution?</li></ul>
Preview next lesson	Examining age and cultural identity.
End positively	Tell the students that it was quite a complex topic today and that they've all done really well.
What the examiners are looking for	Examiners are keen to see that students have a good general knowledge of world sociological events. Encourage the students to use the Internet for research. Use images in colour to prompt and generally be aware that nationality is a contentious subject.
Homework	Ask the students to analyse their findings on nationalism that resulted from their questionnaire.
Getting the most out of your class	Towards the end of a module use concept maps to produce a précis of what is learnt. Split groups up to allow a breadth of ability to complete this map. Place mind map in the classroom (refer to the student book for an example of a mind map, then ask students how they could make it even better!).

Lesson Eleven: Age

Topic	Group	Ability	No. of boys	No. of girls	No. of SEN	Teaching assistant
Identity and age.		AS/A2				

Start positive	Tell the students it was a good lesson on nationality last time.
Connect learning	• Give an example of patriotism. • What is the problem with patriotism? • Contextualise this problem, perhaps using Israel as an example. • What is devolution?
Share learning objectives	• Assess how far age is socially constructed. • Understand the terms 'age' and 'childhood'. • Understand age and the life cycle. • Understand the idea of adolescence.
Lesson outline	Focussing on how age can affect identity.
Starter hook	Ask the students to complete a quiz on legal age limits in England and Wales. (See, for example: http://news.bbc.co.uk/cbbcnews/hi/newsid_3190000/newsid_3190400/3190448. stm).
Activity One	Ask the students if they agree with the age limits in force in England and Wales. Which should be changed? What do they think about the present age of consent for sex? At what age do the students think we become 'adults'?
Activity Two	Ask the students to research stereotypes and how they affect our self concept. Discuss positive concepts of aging; for example, how rising levels of affluence mean that older people are active consumers today.
Activity Three	Debate the idea of adolescence. Is it the most difficult time in our lives? Is waiting so long to be adult a good or bad thing? Who influences us at this time? (Refer to agencies of socialization here.) Has this resulted in sub-cultures that are deviant? How has society responded to these youth cultures?
Review Learning:	• Is age socially constructed? • Give an example of this. • How were things different prior to the industrial revolution? • What is adolescence? • Why is adolescence a particularly difficult time in England and Wales?
Preview next lesson	Looking at disability and sexuality.
End positively	Tell the students it was an interesting lesson looking at age.
What the examiners are looking for	Age allows for many synoptic links to be made. Although this is no longer an essential component of the AS and A2 examination, students should view sociology like an onion that is multi-layered. Clear links can be made here to crime and deviance, education, family, and so on. Students should be encouraged to explain these links when writing assessment essays.
Homework	Ask the students to produce a questionnaire that finds out people's perceptions of age. Is the age of consent in the UK appropriate?
Getting the most out of your class	Building on previous knowledge is a good way to differentiate in terms of difficulty in the classroom. Encourage your students to brainstorm what they know already and then refine and encourage wider and deeper responses.

Lesson Twelve: Disability and sexuality

Topic	Group	Ability	No. of boys	No. of girls	No. of SEN	Teaching assistant
Identity, disability and sexuality.		AS/A2				

Start positive	Tell the students it was a good lesson on age last time.
Connect learning	• Is age socially constructed? Give an example of this. • How were things different prior to the industrial revolution? • What is adolescence? • Why is adolescence a particularly difficult time in England and Wales?
Share learning objectives	• How far disability is socially constructed. • Understand the terms 'disability' and 'sexuality'. • Explain how discrimination on the basis of sexuality or age can affect identity.
Lesson outline	Focussing on how disability and sexuality can affect identity.
Starter hook	Conduct a team quiz covering all the topics studied so far.
Activity One	Conduct a card sort activity in which students match key terms on sexuality to their corresponding definitions. Include terms such as 'homophobia', 'homosexuality', 'heterosexuality' and 'discrimination'. Provide a handout confirming the correct answers.
Activity Two	Discuss with the students how disability and sexuality affects identity. This should cover stereotypes and how they affect our self concept, and positive concepts of disability and sexuality.
Activity Three	Now introduce the Disability Discrimination Act (1995), either through the textbook or by asking students to do Internet research using this link: http://www.direct.gov.uk/en/DisabledPeople/RightsAndObligations/DisabilityRights/index.htm. Discuss how effective this act has been at combating discrimination, and how this affects identity. Explain the idea of disability as a social construct, referring to the social model in the textbook.
Review Learning	• What is homophobia? • How can homophobic bullying affect identity? • Describe the Civil Partnership Act. • How can disability be viewed as a social construct? • How can disability discrimination affect identity?
Preview next lesson	Looking at postmodernism.
End positively	Tell the students there were some interesting issues raised today.
What the examiners are looking for	Students need to be aware that there are many factors affecting identity and that these could affect people in positive or negative ways.
Homework	Ask the students to write an essay examining the effects of age, sexuality and disability on identity (500 words).
Getting the most out of your class	Ask each student to write down one question on a topic they are unsure about. Randomly divide them into small groups and ask them all to give the answer to each other's questions: this will ensure students learn from each other, not just from you.

Lesson Thirteen: Leisure, consumption and identity

Topic	Group	Ability	No. of boys	No. of girls	No. of SEN	Teaching assistant
Postmodernism.		AS/A2				

Start positive	Tell the students it was a good lesson on sexuality and disability last time.
Connect learning	• What is homophobia? • How can homophobic bullying affect identity? • Describe the Civil Partnership Act • How can disability be viewed as a social construct? • How can disability discrimination affect identity?
Share learning objectives	• Understand the term 'postmodernism'. • Apply postmodern theory to leisure and consumption. • Comparing postmodernism to the Marxist views.
Lesson outline	Focussing on our leisure and consumption patterns.
Starter hook	To introduce postmodernism, show students a photo of a soap character, and ask each student to say one word describing the person. Write these on the whiteboard. The students will inevitably describe the soap character not the real person. Now explain that they didn't really tell you anything about the person at all! Ask if they know the real name of the actor. Now link this to the idea that in postmodernity, we can't distinguish between fiction and reality.
Activity One	Give a brief overview of postmodernist theory. This can be achieved through asking students to construct a simple timeline showing premodernity, modernity and postmodernity. Include significant events such as the industrial revolution, the rise of globalisation and the death of the 'meta-narrative'.
Activity Two	Using the textbook, ask students to research information on Baudrillard and his views on shopping and the media. Show pictures of Disneyland to help explain the concept of hyperreality. Ask the students if they think the media creates reality (they will mainly disagree!). Now ask them if they voted during *X factor* or *Big Brother*. Contrast this to the low numbers of people who vote in political elections.
Activity Three	Introduce the postmodern view of cultural hybrids by showing leisure-related images (curry, hip hop music, McDonald's, branded clothing, and so on) and ask the students how a range of cultures and influences shapes our identity and leisure activities.
Activity Four	Assess the postmodern view by asking students to recap their knowledge of Marxism. Link this to leisure, by re-introducing notions of false consciousness, false needs and leisure and consumption as helping the economy.
Review learning	• Describe postmodern society • What is a meta-narrative? • What does Baudrillard say about leisure and shopping? • What do Marxists think about leisure and consumption? • State one other criticism of postmodernism.
End positively	Tell the students that you're really impressed at how well they all understood postmodernism.
What the examiners are looking for	Students need a basic understanding of postmodernism at AS level. The examiners like to see reference to a range of modern theorists and evidence.
Homework	Revise for a mock exam on culture and identity to be held next lesson.
Getting the most out of your class	AS students will find the concepts of postmodernism and postmodernity challenging, so this lesson could be spread over two hours or more if needed. Reassure them that even undergraduate sociology students find this topic difficult!

Lesson One: Different definitions and ways of measuring wealth, poverty and welfare

Topic	Group	Ability	No. of boys	No. of girls	No. of SEN	Teaching assistant
Defining and measuring poverty.		AS				

Start positive	Tell the students it was a great lesson last time.
Connect learning	• What is happening to birth rates? • When and where they at their highest and lowest? • Explain the trend in mortality rates. • Explain trends in fertility.
Share learning objectives	• List different definitions of poverty. • Show an understanding of why different methods are used. • Outline how poverty is measured. • Be aware of the strengths and weaknesses of the different approaches and definitions and measurement of poverty. • Be aware of the amount of poverty in the UK.
Lesson outline	Looking at the definitions and measurements of poverty.
Starter hook	Write down your own definitions of poverty. This should naturally result in some disagreement, which can be resolved by explaining that there are several types of poverty.
Activity One	Use a card sort activity in which the students work in groups to match types of poverty (absolute, relative and social exclusion) with their definitions. This can be extended by adding key concepts such as 'subjectivity', 'poverty line', 'deprivation index', 'wealth', 'income', etc. The answers could either be noted by students in a poverty glossary or given out as a handout.
Activity Two	Ask the students to compile a list of non-necessities in a modern twenty-first century home. Ask them to make a similar list for 20 years ago. What differences would there be? Ask them to indicate the non-essentials in 20 years' time, and so on. Now introduce the key studies that have aimed to measure poverty (Rowntree's study of absolute poverty, Townsend's study of relative poverty and the *Social Exclusion* list). Ask students to make criticisms of these studies.
Activity Three	Use the following link for the *Poverty and Social Exclusion* list (Joseph Rowntree Foundation): http://www.jrf.org.uk/knowledge/findings/socialpolicy/930.asp. Ask the students to tick the items they think are necessities and then compare their lists with their classmates. Which items is there agreement about? Which are more problematic? Ask the students to compare the findings of the 2000 survey with their own. Numbers 1–35 on the list were considered essential by 50 per cent or more of the households, whilst two out of three classified 1–25 as necessities. Do the students agree with these findings? Summarise by looking at problems with using both the absolute and relative definitions. Ask the students to research problems of defining and measuring wealth and income.
Activity Four	Use the *Times Rich List* (http://business.timesonline.co.uk/tol/business/specials/rich_list/rich_list_search/) to find out the estimated wealth of famous people. Show pictures of them to the students and ask them to guess how wealthy they are. They will probably grossly underestimate, which will help them understand the unequal distribution of wealth in the UK.
Review learning	• What is absolute poverty? Give an advantage of such a definition. Give an example. • What is relative poverty? Give an advantage of such a definition. Give an example. • Give disadvantages of absolute and relative poverty.
Preview next lesson	Looking at poverty on a more global scale.

Lesson 1

End positively	Tell the students it was a really good start to the module.
What the examiners are looking for	Questions come up in terms of the difference between income and wealth: wealth as a stock, and income as a flow of assets. There are also questions on what 'relative poverty' is.
Homework	Ask the students to record their 'cost of living' for one week. They should calculate costs of their food, leisure activities, etc.
Getting the most out of your class	Explain to the students that in reality neither relative nor absolute definitions of poverty offer a complete definition of poverty. What is far more important is that the students understand the problems and advantages of each measurement technique.

Lesson Two: Different definitions and ways of measuring wealth, poverty and welfare

Topic	Group	Ability	No. of boys	No. of girls	No. of SEN	Teaching assistant
World poverty.		AS				

Start positive	Tell the students that it was an excellent lesson looking at definitions of poverty last time.
Connect learning	• What is absolute poverty? Give an advantage of such a definition. • Give an example of absolute poverty. • What is relative poverty? Give an advantage of such a definition. • Give an example of relative poverty. • Give disadvantages of absolute and relative poverty.
Share learning objectives	• Research poverty across the UK and compare it with world poverty. • Learn that all poverty is relative.
Lesson outline	Looking at poverty across the globe.
Starter hook	Show images of children in poor or Third World countries.
Activity One	Ask your students to go to the Townsend Centre for International Poverty website (http://www.bristol.ac.uk/poverty/news.html) and the Make Poverty History website (http://www.makepovertyhistory.org/). Ask the students to work in groups of three and produce a presentation outlining poverty within the UK, contrasting it to poverty across the globe. This can be presented in terms of images, facts, video clips, presentations, and so on.
Activity Two	Ask the students to research poverty in a country of their choice by continent (for example, Asia: Bangladesh, India; Africa: Kenya, Rwanda; Latin America: Mexico, Honduras; Europe: Russia, etc.) Variables to be explored include: life expectancy, child mortality, average calorific intake, literacy rates, children in the labour force, access to clean water, and so on.
Review learning	• Which continent is the poorest? • What is happening to poverty as a general trend across the world? Give one reason for this. • Give a reason for researching the poverty of the country you chose.
Preview next lesson	Looking at the links between poverty and different social groups.
End positively	Tell the students they carried out excellent research today.
What the examiners are looking for	All examiners like to see that the nominal A level Sociology candidate has a keen eye for world issues and is aware of what is going on around them. Although specific knowledge is not a particular requirement, it is desirable.
Homework	Ask the students to produce a set of graphs, tables and images that summarise their findings on a country of their choice.
Getting the most out of your class	Encourage all students to read a quality newspaper. You can encourage this by contacting the newspapers and asking for special offers for sixth form students. The *Times* and the *Guardian* both run student schemes. Secondly, bring newspapers and magazines into the classroom, leave them on a side table and encourage students to read them during breaks and so on. *Sociology Review* and *New Internationalist* are useful magazines.

Lesson Three: The distribution of poverty, wealth and income between different social groups

Topic	Group	Ability	No. of boys	No. of girls	No. of SEN	Teaching assistant
Who are the 'poor'?		AS				

Start positive	Tell the students it was a good lesson on comparisons of poverty across the world last time.
Connect learning	• Which continent is the poorest? • What is happening to poverty as a general trend across the world? Give one reason for this. • Explain one reason for your chosen case studies poverty.
Share learning objectives	• Identify groups who make up the poor in the UK. • Explain why these groups are in poverty. • Relate different theories to explain this poverty.
Lesson outline	An assessment of the groups most likely to be in poverty in the UK.
Starter hook	Ask the students to write down who they think make up the poor. Ask them to think about social class, ethnic group, age group, gender and how locality affects poverty.
Activity One	Research how class is measured in the UK. (To see the eight official social classes in the UK use: http://www.statistics.gov.uk/methods_quality/ns_sec/cat_desc_op_issue.asp). Which socio-economic classes do they think are most likely to have the lowest income? Why is this? Ask them to complete a table explaining the income of the social classes. Ask the students to present this in diagrammatical form on a poster. Each poster should include pen pictures of those from different classes, with the name of the person, income, education, diet, occupation, time spent unemployed, job satisfaction, and so on.
Activity Two	Ask the students to research childhood and poverty. What is the general trend for childhood poverty? What is the government target for reducing childhood poverty? Has it been reached? Which family types are most likely to lead to childhood poverty? How does poverty individually affect children?
Activity Three	Ask the students to produce a report on why women are more likely to live in poverty than men. Get them to think of the following: their income, why other factors impinge on economic success, types of job women do, the glass ceiling, etc.
Review learning	• Name one group that is most likely to suffer from poverty. Give a brief explanation of this. • How do sociologists measure class? • Which class is most likely to suffer from poverty? • Explain which family grouping tends to suffer from poverty.
Preview next lesson	Looking at the persistence of poverty in contemporary society.
End positively	Tell the students that it was another great lesson.
What the examiners are looking for	Students will often be required to, for example, give three reasons why one group is in poverty. Answers are similar for all groups; that is, low pay, high unemployment, sex discrimination, lower educational qualifications, language barriers, and so on.
Homework	Using at least two different textbooks, find three possible reasons why each of the following social groups are likely to experience poverty: ethnic minority groups, people with disabilities, one-parent families and pensioners.
Getting the most out of your class	Encourage the students to use their own personal experiences of discrimination. For example, if your school has a high ethnic mix, focus on the group concerned and how discrimination affects them.

Lesson Four: The existence and persistence of poverty in contemporary society

Topic	Group	Ability	No. of boys	No. of girls	No. of SEN	Teaching assistant
The existence and persistence of poverty: cultural explanations.		AS				

Start positive	Tell the students it was a good lesson looking at social class and poverty last time.
Connect learning	• Provide one group that is most likely to suffer from poverty. Give a brief explanation of this. • How do sociologists measure social class? • Which social class is most likely to suffer from poverty? • Explain which family grouping tends to suffer from poverty.
Share learning objectives	• Explain and outline competing ideologies on poverty. • Look at why poverty remains so constant. • Evaluate the New Right perspectives on poverty. • Evaluate other cultural explanations of poverty
Lesson outline	An assessment of the different theories of poverty.
Starter hook	Ask the students to write down five reasons why they think poverty continues to be a major issue in contemporary society.
Activity One	Students will need a brief explanation of the difference between 'left wing' and 'right wing' to fully understand this topic. You can then introduce the point that right wing explanations of poverty usually blame the individual's culture or behaviour for their poverty, and are therefore known as 'cultural' or 'sub-cultural' explanations. To assess the work of Oscar Lewis, it is interesting to look at the so called working-class 'culture'. Ask the students to research what working-class culture is all about. In particular ask them to assess the working-class perspective on life. Ask them to interview their grandparents or anyone they know who has been part of the working classes in their lifetime. This can be presented as a collage, a mobile, and so on.
Activity Two	Now introduce Murray's controversial study on the underclass (for his original articles see: www.civitas.org.uk/pdf/cw33.pdf and www.civitas.org.uk/pdf/cs10.pdf). Invite students to evaluate this theory of why poverty exists (a heated argument could occur!). If this is the first time that students have encountered the New Right perspective, then a basic explanation will be required.
Review learning	• How does the 'culture of poverty' explanation describe poverty? • How do the New Right view poverty? What explanations do they suggest? • For each theory give one strength and one weakness of their arguments. • Why are these theories also known as cultural explanations of poverty?
Preview next lesson	Looking at how other types of sociologists explain poverty.
End positively	Tell the students that you are impressed at how well they've worked today.
What the examiners are looking for	For lower-mark questions students are often expected to know the disadvantages of each theoretical explanation of poverty, or they expect students to write an essay on assessing the sociological explanations of poverty. Students are expected to use their full 'tool kit' of theories to answer this type of question.
Homework	Ask the students to extend their knowledge of Murray's views on the underclass by reading parts of his original article at: www.civitas.org.uk/pdf/cw33.pdf. Ask them to write a summary of his views in their sociology journal.
Getting the most out of your class	The 'tool kit' is an important way of explaining concepts to students. Why not produce a crib sheet that explains all the theories of poverty, wealth and welfare in tabular form? Include key writers, concepts, theories, and strengths and weaknesses. Remember to also include images as some students learn better visually rather than using words. Nearer to the examination test the students regularly.

Lesson Five: The existence and persistence of poverty in contemporary society

Topic	Group	Ability	No. of boys	No. of girls	No. of SEN	Teaching assistant
The existence and persistence of poverty: structural explanations.		AS				

Start positive	An excellent lesson on the different theoretical explanations of poverty.
Connect learning	<ul><li>How does the 'culture of poverty' explanation explain poverty?</li><li>How do the New Right see poverty? What explanations do they suggest?</li><li>For each theory give one strength and one weakness of the arguments.</li><li>Why are these theories also known as cultural explanations of poverty?</li></ul>
Share learning objectives	<ul><li>Explain and outline competing ideologies on poverty.</li><li>Look at why poverty remains so persistent.</li><li>Evaluate Marxist explanations of poverty.</li><li>Evaluate the social democratic views on poverty.</li></ul>
Lesson outline	Continuing the assessment of the different theories of poverty.
Starter hook	Ask the students about child care in this country. Is it free? Is it available full time? If a person can't afford it can they still work? Ask them what they think the national minimum wage is: how much would a worker earn each week after tax? How much could the students spend on one night out?.
Activity One	Remind the students what left wing means. Explain that left-wing explanations of poverty usually blame society for poverty. Introduce the social democratic explanation of welfare using Frank Field's theory that the underclass is caused by the poverty trap. Students could use the Internet to research the monetary values of the key benefits available and the current rates of the national minimum wage. They could also find examples of nursery fees by looking at the websites of local nurseries. (Useful websites include: http://www.hmrc.gov.uk/nmw/ and http://www.direct.gov.uk.)
Activity Two	Introduce the Marxist explanation of poverty. As before, if this is the first time your students will learn about Marxism, an introduction will be needed (see the ideas in the *culture and identity* topic). If you have already covered Marxism, give each student a card or sticky note, each containing a key Marxist concept ('bourgeoisie', 'proletariat', 'capitalism', 'communism', 'exploitation', 'means of production', and so on). Each student should try to talk about their concept for one minute. Now link this to poverty, keeping it simplistic.
Activity Three	A good way to look at competing theories of poverty is to split the students into the different ideologies. Produce a set of card prompts on each theory. Ask the students to present each theory explaining key writers, concepts, strengths and weaknesses of each theory. This can be presented in a number of formats: a presentation, a large tabular summary, a set of images, a mobile, and so on.
Review learning	<ul><li>Name two society-based explanations of poverty.</li><li>Explain what is meant by the poverty trap.</li><li>Give two criticisms of the Marxist view of poverty.</li><li>What are the differences between Murray's underclass and Field's underclass?</li></ul>
Preview next lesson	Looking at how poverty has been tackled by social policy.
End positively	Tell the students you really enjoyed this lesson. Ask them if they enjoyed it too.
What the examiners are looking for	For lower-mark questions students are often expected to know the disadvantages of each theoretical explanation of poverty, or students are expected to write an essay on assessing the sub-cultural explanations of poverty. Students are expected to use their full tool kit of theories to answer this type of question.
Homework	Set an essay: 'Assess sociological explanations of poverty in modern society'.
Getting the most out of your class	Why not ask the students to devise quiz questions? Divide them into two teams and ask each team to write five questions to test their opponents. You can specify the topics that the questions should be based around.

Lesson Six: Different responses to poverty, with particular reference to the role of social policy since the 1940s

Topic	Group	Ability	No. of boys	No. of girls	No. of SEN	Teaching assistant
The role of social policy since the 1940s.		AS				

Start positive	Tell the students you had an excellent lesson on the different theoretical explanations of poverty last time.
Connect learning	<ul><li>How does the 'culture of poverty' explanation explain poverty?</li><li>How does the New Right see poverty? What explanations do they suggest?</li><li>For each theory give one strength and one weakness of their arguments.</li><li>How do Marxists explain poverty?</li><li>How do feminists explain poverty amongst women?</li></ul>
Share learning objectives	<ul><li>Define what the welfare state is.</li><li>Look at examples of social policy.</li><li>Assess the effectiveness of such policies on differing social groups.</li></ul>
Lesson outline	Looking at social policy initiatives to tackle poverty.
Starter hook	Ask the students to write down as many examples of social policy that they can think of.
Activity One	One way to see how social policy has progressed over time is by using a timeline. Ask the students to produce a timeline starting with 1940 and take it up to the present day. Ask them to add appropriate laws and policies introduced for each date and add appropriate images. Divide the timeline into three main stages: the post-war era, the New Right era and the current New Labour era. Display in the classroom and refer back to it as either an aide memoir or as a diagnostic tool.
Activity Two	For each appropriate group ask the students to produce an assessment of how far social policy has lifted that social group out of poverty. Ask them to choose from ethnic minorities, women, the working classes, single parent families, and so on.
Activity Three	Ask students to recall all the theories of poverty learned during the last two lessons. For each one, students should decide how that perspective or theory would solve poverty. Use textbooks if needed. Prompt your students to link their ideas to the role of social policy (that is, social democrats would increase benefits and wages, whilst Murray would eliminate all benefits for unmarried women!).
Review learning	<ul><li>When the welfare state was first introduced?</li><li>What was the workhouse?</li><li>Who was Beveridge?</li><li>Give one theoretical perspective on welfare?</li><li>Give one strength of this perspective.</li><li>Give a weakness of this perspective.</li></ul>
Preview next lesson	Looking at the nature and role of public, private, voluntary and informal welfare provision.
End positively	Tell the students it was another enjoyable lesson.
What the examiners are looking for	On occasions examiners use a phrase to see how students cope with it. Ensure you talk about some of the stock phrases used within social policy: 'means testing', 'universalism', 'selectivism', and so on.
Homework	Give students a copy of Gans' article on 'the functions of poverty' (found at http://www.sociology.org.uk/as4p3.pdf). Ask them to review the article in their sociology journal, deciding whether they agree with each function. They should conclude by deciding whether poverty really needs to be solved!
Getting the most out of your class	A good way for your students to get to grips with key phrases is for them to write out key words on card and then place them around the classroom. Ask them to use images to help them remember them. You can then use these at the start of a lesson, asking each pupil to explain as many as they can in 60 seconds or just use it as a starter for the lesson.

Lesson Seven: The nature and the role of the public, private, voluntary and informal welfare provision in contemporary society

Topic	Group	Ability	No. of boys	No. of girls	No. of SEN	Teaching assistant
Welfare pluralism (the mixed economy of welfare).		AS				

Start positive	Tell the students it was an excellent lesson last time.
Connect learning	<ul><li>When was the welfare state first introduced?</li><li>Who was Beveridge?</li><li>Give one theoretical perspective on welfare.</li><li>Give one strength of this perspective.</li><li>Give a weakness of this perspective.</li></ul>
Share learning objectives	<ul><li>Look at current welfare provision in the UK.</li><li>Explain what is meant by 'welfare pluralism'.</li><li>Assess the role of private, informal and voluntary welfare provision.</li></ul>
Lesson outline	An assessment of the welfare regimes across Europe in comparison to the UK.
Starter hook	Ask the students what 'welfare' means. Who provides their welfare? Try to prompt answers such as 'schools', 'parents', 'charities' and 'the government'.
Activity One	On an overhead projector show two columns: the left column should contain a list of key concepts for this lesson (welfare pluralism, mixed economy of welfare, informal welfare, private welfare, statutory welfare, means-testing, universalism, and so on). The right column should contain all the definitions but in the wrong order. Ask the students to identify the correct matching pairs, and then add the definitions to their poverty glossary.
Activity Two	Provide handouts or use the textbook to give more information about the four sources of welfare used today. Link this to the ideology of New Labour (that is, the government advocates the Third Way in welfare provision, uses a mixture of universal and means-tested benefits and uses a variety of welfare providers).
Activity Three	Host a formal debate that draws together all of the recent lessons on welfare and policy, such as 'Should benefits be means-tested or universal?' Ask students to form two teams, each with a team captain. Give them time to prepare their side of the debate, then make a rule that everyone must contribute at least once. You could make the captains responsible for controlling unruly behaviour such as shouting or interrupting.
Review learning	<ul><li>What is welfare pluralism?</li><li>What are the four providers of welfare in the UK?</li><li>Suggest two problems of using private welfare..</li><li>Suggest two advantages of using voluntary organisations.</li></ul>
End positively	Tell the students that this was a great module.
What the examiners are looking for	As sociology moves into a global environment, examiners want to see that students have an eclectic knowledge of the world around them. They expect this in any nominal 18-year-old student as it shows that the student is absorbing and using their sociology in a useful and challenging way.
Homework	Ask the students to revise this module ready for a mock exam next lesson.
Getting the most out of your class	Although the Internet is a fantastic resource centre for A level students please make them aware of its limitations. You should advise them on the most appropriate websites. As with everything on the Internet, quality is variable: anyone can post articles. They need to look for websites that are written by both academics and teachers who know what they need to know for their examination. Moreover, find websites convey this knowledge in the plainest and most accessible form.

Families and households

Lesson One: Introduction

Topic	Group	Ability	No. of boys	No. of girls	No. of SEN	Teaching assistant
Ice-breaker lesson: Introducing the family.		AS				

Start positive	Explain to the students that we are all members of a family. Thus we all have an insight into the workings and function of the family unit.
Connect learning	If you are teaching two topics from Unit One, ask the students to use the whiteboard to put links between culture, identity and poverty and the family. For example, socialization. What role does the family play in this?
Share learning objectives	• Understand the problems with defining the family. • Understand the different family types. • Explain the advantages and disadvantages of these types.
Lesson outline	An exploration of what the family is and its functions.
Starter hook	Use images of a single-parent family, a nuclear family, an extended family, a same sex family, and so on. You could use fictional or celebrity families such as *The Simpsons*, *Family Guy* or the royal family. Ask your students to make a few comments on paper or a whiteboard answering the following questions: Is this a family? What are the advantages of this family type? What are the disadvantages of this family type?
Activity One	Ask the students to comment on their family. Compare and contrast the other family types that emerge. One way to do this is through the 'triad system'. Have a scribe, interviewer and interviewee. Ask each to spend 10 minutes on each task, with the scribe taking notes.
Activity Two	Put George Peter Murdock's definition of the family on the overhead projector. Point out that it contains four functions that a family performs. Ask the students what is wrong with the definition. Think of other family types that do not conform to this definition. Make a list of these families; prompting students where necessary. Ask the students to write definitions for each family type, using textbooks and sociology dictionaries where needed. As an extension, ask them to research concepts that will not come up in the discussion (matrifocal, polygyny, polygamy and polyandry).
Activity Three	Ask your students to construct a questionnaire on the different types of families they live in. Ask them to think about how they are going to operationalise this idea. Also get them to isolate the experiences of these different types of family.
Review learning	• Who came up with the definitive definition of the family? • Provide one type of family. • What are the functions of the family? • Explain one problem with the family.
Preview next lesson	Examining the family and social structure.
End positively	Tell the students it was a really good start to the module. Tell them well done!
What the examiners are looking for	Questions are often asked on why students think different family types are important.
Homework	Ask the students to ask their parents to complete their questionnaires.
Getting the most out of your class	Even at this stage in the course, ask students to remember sociologists such as Murdock and Parsons. Use concept walls or give mini tests at the start of lessons.

Lesson Two: The relationship of the family to the social structure and the economy

Topic	Group	Ability	No. of boys	No. of girls	No. of SEN	Teaching assistant
The relationship of the family to the social structure: the functionalist and New Right views.		AS				

Start positive	Tell the students it was an excellent lesson on definitions of the family last time.
Connect learning	• Give one definition of the family. • Give examples that explain a family type. • Give some functions of the family.
Share learning objectives	• Understand functionalist and New Right theories of the family. • Quote appropriate writers for each theory. • Understand what each theory suggests. • Evaluate each theory effectively.
Lesson outline	An assessment of two key theories of the family.
Starter hook	One way to introduce this is by using a graffiti board. Split your class into two groups and allocate one theory of the family to each of them. Get them to produce a wall that depicts what they think different theorists might say.
Activity One	If this is the first time you will be teaching theory to your students, they will need considerable time spent introducing the perspectives in general: see the lesson plans on *culture and identity* for ideas. Introduce key functionalists (Murdock, Parsons) and the key New Right theorist (Murray). Explain how they see the (nuclear) family as an important part of the social structure of society. Write the names of key writers or concepts on individual cards (or use images of the writers) and their theories on separate cards. Ask the students to match the writers or concepts with the theories. This helps to engage both picture and other memory types. You can also use these words as a revision game.
Activity Two	Ask the students to use the textbook or a handout to produce a mobile showing images of key writers, concepts, strengths and weaknesses, and so on.
Activity Three	Produce a list of strengths and criticisms for each theory covered in the lesson. Then ask the students to isolate which theory it is a strength or criticism of. This teaches the importance of evaluation.
Review learning	• Name two perspectives that support the nuclear family. • Name an appropriate writer for each theory. • Give a strength of each theory. • Give a weakness of each theory.
Preview next lesson	Looking at industrialisation and the family.
End positively	Tell the students it was an excellent lesson on theories of the family.
What the examiners are looking for	Examiners like to ask questions that allow students use of the theories they have learned.
Homework	Set the students a mini-essay: Examine the different functions performed by the family for individuals and for society (250–500 words).
Getting the most out of your class	Hold regular tests, particularly on major theorists.

Lesson Three: The relationship of the family to the social structure and the economy

Topic	Group	Ability	No. of boys	No. of girls	No. of SEN	Teaching assistant
The relationship of the family to the social structure: the Marxist and feminist views.		AS				

Start positive	Ask the students if they can tackle Marxism and feminism as well as they tackled functionalism and the New Right.
Connect learning	• Give an overview of the functionalist view of the family. • Give one criticism of the functionalist view. • Briefly explain the key ideas of New Right sociologists. • What does Murray say about the UK 'underclass'?
Share learning objectives	• Understand Marxist and feminist theories of the family. • Quote appropriate writers for each theory. • Understand what each theory suggests. • Evaluate each theory effectively.
Lesson outline	An assessment of two more key theories of the family.
Starter hook	Write some quotes and key views of feminists and Marxists on the whiteboard. For example, "Wives play their traditional role as takers of sh*t" (Ansley, 1972) and "Families support capitalism by producing future workers to be exploited" (Zaretsky, 1976) to spark initial interest. Ask the students to name the perspective associated with each phrase and explore what Marxists and feminists might say about the family.
Activity One	If this is the first time you will be teaching theory to your students, they will need considerable time spent introducing the perspectives in general. Introduce key Marxists (Engels and Zaretsky) and feminists (Ansley, Delphy and Leonard). Explain how they see the family as contributing to, and maintaining, the existing social structure. Either cut up images of key writers or write down concepts on pieces of card. Write down matching theories on separate pieces of card. Ask the students to match the images or concepts with the appropriate theories. This helps engage both picture and other memory types. You can also use these words as a revision game.
Activity Two	Ask the students to use the textbook or a handout to produce a mobile showing images of key writers, concepts, strengths and weaknesses, and son on. Display the mobile in classroom.
Activity Three	Produce a list of strengths and criticisms as a handout for each theory covered in the lesson. Then ask the students to isolate which theory they are strengths or criticisms of and whether they are strengths or weaknesses. This is important as it teaches the importance of evaluation.
Review learning	• What is a 'conflict perspective'? • Name two sociological perspectives that are critical of families. • Give a strength of each perspective. • Give a weakness of each perspective.
Preview next lesson	Looking at policies affecting the family.
End positively	Tell the students it was an excellent lesson on theories of the family.
What the examiners are looking for	Examiners increasingly like to ask questions that allow students to use the theories they have learned. For example, 'Examine the contribution of feminism to your understanding of the family.'
Homework	Produce a poster separated into four sections showing functionalist, New Right, feminist and Marxist views of the family. Ask the students to include criticisms of each perspective.
Getting the most out of your class	Have regular tests, particularly on major theorists.

Lesson Four: The relationship of the family to the social structure and the economy

Topic	Group	Ability	No. of boys	No. of girls	No. of SEN	Teaching assistant
Social policy and the family.						
Start positive	Tell the students that they're doing really well in this module so far.					
Connect learning	<ul><li>What is the 'fit thesis'?</li><li>Which writer is most associated with this theory?</li><li>Name writers who criticise this theory.</li><li>What methodological criticisms can be made of these writers?</li></ul>					
Share learning objectives	<ul><li>Understand what is meant by social policy.</li><li>List and describe three social policies.</li><li>Explain how these social policies affect families.</li></ul>					
Lesson outline	An assessment of two more key theories of the family.					
Starter hook	Using the whiteboard, initiate a game of hangman; the answer being 'social policy'. Ask the students to explore what this might mean, then ask for examples of policies they might have heard of.					
Activity One	Introduce SureStart to the students – this can be done by means of a simple presentation or by distributing recent copies of the SureStart magazine (you can subscribe to this free of charge at: http://www.surestart.gov.uk/magazine/). The main points to include are the provision of parenting classes or drop-in centres and the weekly twelve-and-a-half free hours' of nursery for young children. Initiate a discussion on how this affects families (prompt them to think of working parents and whether the amount of free nursery school is enough).					
Activity Two	Introduce child tax credit. (This can be done by providing handouts of information from: http://www.direct.gov.uk/en/MoneyTaxAndBenefits/TaxCreditsandChildBenefit/TaxCredits/DG_073802.) Ask the students to assess the impact of this policy on families (prompt them to raise issues such as increased affluence, incentives for both parents to work, and so on).					
Activity Three	Ask the students what they know about maternity and paternity leave. Show them the current entitlements for men and women (http://www.direct.gov.uk/en/Dioll/EmploymentInteractiveTools/DG_065384) and ask them to evaluate the effects on families. A mini-debate could be held on whether men should have the same amount of time off work as women when they have a baby.					
Review learning	<ul><li>What is a social policy?</li><li>List three current social policies.</li><li>Explain what tax credits are.</li><li>How significant is SureStart to families?</li></ul>					
Preview next lesson	Looking at the decline of the nuclear family.					
End positively	Tell the students this was an excellent lesson on policies.					
What the examiners are looking for	Examiners like students to use modern-day examples in their answers. Policies are continually being updated or replaced; meaning textbooks are of limited use for this lesson. Remind your students to read the society section of newspapers regularly in case any relevant new policies are introduced.					
Homework	Ask the students to use the Internet to find information on two more social policies: the Divorce Reform Act 1969 and the Civil Partnership Act 2005.					
Getting the most out of your class	To motivate kinaesthetic learners, ask students to produce a three-minute play showing how a social policy affects a family.					

Lesson Five: Changing patterns of marriage, cohabitation, separation, divorce, child-bearing and the life-course

Topic	Group	Ability	No. of boys	No. of girls	No. of SEN	Teaching assistant
Is the traditional nuclear family in crisis?		AS				

Start positive	Tell the students it was a good lesson looking at policies affecting the family last time.
Connect learning	<ul><li>Define 'social policy'.</li><li>Explain how changes in divorce laws have affected family diversity.</li><li>Explain how new legislation on civil partnerships has affected family diversity.</li><li>List three benefits available to families.</li><li>Summarise the key sociological perspectives' views on social policy.</li></ul>
Share learning objectives	<ul><li>Isolate trends to suggest that the traditional nuclear family is in crisis.</li><li>Examine the reasons for these trends.</li><li>Be aware of the role in social policy in formation of this crisis.</li><li>Consider what can be done in the future to change the perception of the family and to reduce this apparent crisis.</li></ul>
Lesson outline	Identifying reasons that suggest a decline in the family and isolating the trends that are occurring in contemporary Great Britain to suggest this.
Starter hook	Hand out images of some of the key concepts and ask the students to think of what trends are occurring with each example.
Activity One	Suggest to your students that the family is under attack or decline. Ask the students to identity factors that would suggest this to be the case.
Activity Two	Give the students a range of statistics on marriage, cohabitation, separation, divorce, child bearing and family diversity (use textbooks or social trends data: http://www.statistics.gov.uk/StatBase/Product.asp?vlnk = 5748). Ask the students to come up with a set of hypotheses that explain what is happening to the contemporary family in the UK.
Activity Three	Sort your students into groups and ask them to research these trends in more depth. Use a wide range of websites, including Office for National Statistics and the Cabinet Office, and ask the students to report back their findings in a presentation. Specifically, ask them to look at present social policy and ask them to hypothesise whether social policy will need to change in the face of the present trends. It may be useful to produce a worksheet including all the key questions you want them to answer. Aim to include questions on: changes in the marriage and divorce rates, the popularity of cohabitation, the average number of children per family and the average age of childbirth among women.
Review learning	<ul><li>Give one indication that the family is in crisis.</li><li>Give one reason why people are cohabiting rather than marrying.</li><li>What is happening to the divorce rate?</li><li>Why are women having fewer children?</li><li>Why are there more one-parent families than there used to be?</li><li>Give another family structure that you are aware of.</li></ul>
Preview next lesson	Focusing on sociological explanations of divorce next lesson.
End positively	Tell the students that they've covered a lot today. Tell them well done.
What the examiners are looking for	The examiners want students to be aware of contemporary trends within the family. They particularly like asking about trends in family structure such as the nuclear family, the extended family and one-parent families.
Homework	Activity Three may well take place over more than one lesson. Alternatively, let the groups work on their presentations for homework.
Getting the most out of your class	When undertaking work on the family it is ideal to use images from your students' families and to link these to theory and sociological detail

Lesson Six: Changing patterns of marriage, cohabitation, separation, divorce, child-bearing and the life-course

Topic	Group	Ability	No. of boys	No. of girls	No. of SEN	Teaching assistant
Theories of divorce		AS				

Start positive	Tell the students it was a good lesson last time on trends that are occurring in the family in the UK.
Connect learning	• Give one indication that the family is in crisis. • Give one reason why people are cohabiting rather than marrying. • What is happening to the divorce rate? • Why are women having fewer children? • Why are there more one-parent families? • Give another family structure that you are aware of.
Share learning objectives	• Understand contemporary trends in divorce in the UK. • Understand sociological reasons for divorce. • Understand potential long-term trends in divorce and social policy that might be used to tackle this.
Lesson outline	Looking at trends in divorce rates in the UK and the reasons for this.
Starter hook	Give the students some long-term statistics on the divorce rate in the UK. They may have found these themselves during the previous lesson. Ask them to isolate appropriate trends in pairs.
Activity One	Give the students a list of reasons why the divorce rate has increased in the UK (for examples, changes in the law, the impact of feminism, changing norms and values in society, secularisation and the increased value of marriage). With each example, try to get your students to think how this might affect the divorce rate.
Activity Two	Give students a chance to research a particular area of divorce. For example, legislation (ask them to produce a timeline explaining laws and their affect). Why are women more likely to initiate a divorce petition? Why are divorce rates so high for teenagers, for those who have been married for around 20 years and for those from different cultural or social backgrounds? Ensure they evaluate their chosen theory (they may need help with this).
Activity Three	To involve research ask your students to interview their parents or grandparents to ascertain what makes a happy long-lasting marriage.
Review learning	• What is happening to the long-term divorce rate in the UK? • What is the recent trend in divorce rates? • Give reasons why the divorce rate has increased. • Give a sociological reason for the increasing divorce rate.
Preview next lesson	Looking at diversity in the UK family structure.
End positively	Tell the students it was an excellent lesson on divorce.
What the examiners are looking for	Examiners often ask for reasons for the increase in the divorce rate. This may include general questions or more specific ones; for example, on legislation.
Homework	Set the students an essay: Using material from Item 1B and elsewhere, assess sociological explanations of the increase in the number of divorces since the 1960s (300–600 words).
Getting the most out of your class	It is very important that sociology teachers keep up with current trends, particularly when it comes to contemporary material such as divorce rates, cohabitation rates, and so on. These can be easily accessed by looking at, for example, social trends (http://www.statistics.gov. uk/statbase/Product.asp?vlnk = 5748&More = N).

Lesson Seven: The diversity of contemporary family and household structures

Topic	Group	Ability	No. of boys	No. of girls	No. of SEN	Teaching assistant
Family diversity.		AS				

Start positive	Tell the students it was an excellent lesson last time.
Connect learning	<ul><li>What is happening to the long-term divorce rate in the UK?</li><li>What is the recent trend in divorce rates?</li><li>Give reasons why the divorce rate has increased.</li><li>Give a sociological reason for the increasing divorce rate.</li></ul>
Share learning objectives	<ul><li>Understand the diversity in family structure in the UK.</li><li>Understand the different family types by group.</li><li>Understand different sociological explanations of whether the nuclear family is dominant in UK society.</li></ul>
Lesson outline	Focussing on whether the nuclear family is still universal.
Starter hook	Give the students a recap quiz that draws together students' existing knowledge on this topic. Include questions on Murdock, types of families and their recent research on current family trends.
Activity One	Ask students to summarise trends they found on diversity in the family. Use all up-to-date material such as social trends and the Office for National Statistics.
Activity Two	Introduce key studies on family diversity such as Rapoport's categories of diversity and Eversley and Bonnerjea's work on regional/geographical diversity. Contrast these to sociologists who believe diversity is limited (such as Chester's work on the neo-conventional family). You could use a number of different activities. Ask the students to draw a timeline, paced out in decades, recording the changes in family structure, key writers, key trends, and so on.
Activity Three	Summarise sociological perspectives on family diversity. This will help students revise their knowledge of functionalism, New Right, Marxism and feminism.
Review learning	<ul><li>Comment upon changes in family structure in the UK.</li><li>Give one example of diversity in UK family structure.</li><li>Comment upon feminist and New Right views of diversity.</li><li>Give an example of locational diversity.</li><li>Give an example of cultural diversity.</li><li>Explain postmodern arguments of diversity.</li></ul>
Preview next lesson	Looking at the diversity of the contemporary family and household structures.
End positively	Tell the students it was an excellent lesson on diversity.
What the examiners are looking for	Examiners like to ask the reasons why families are becoming more diverse and to ask students to compare evidence for the decline of the nuclear family for an increasingly diverse family structure.
Homework	Ask the students to prepare a detailed essay plan that addresses the following question: Assess the view that, despite recent changes in family life, the conventional nuclear family remains the norm for families and households in Britain today.
Getting the most out of your class	One way to encourage students is to get them into the 'field'. Why not ask them to interview families for homework? What family structures are dominant in the area around your school or college?

Lesson 8

Lesson Eight: The diversity of contemporary family and household structures

Topic	Group	Ability	No. of boys	No. of girls	No. of SEN	Teaching assistant
One-parent families.		AS				

Start positive	Tell the students it was an excellent lesson on family diversity in the UK last time.
Connect learning	• Comment upon changes in family structure in the UK. • Give one example of diversity in UK family structure. • Comment upon feminist and New Right views of diversity. • Give an example of locational diversity. • Give an example of cultural diversity. • Explain postmodern arguments of diversity.
Share learning objectives	• Understand contemporary trends in the formation of one-parent families. • Comprehend the advantages and disadvantages of this grouping. • Be aware of factors that have led to the development of one-parent families. • Be able to explain sociological explanations for the formation of one-parent families.
Lesson outline	An assessment of the quantity, quality and reasons of formation of one-parent families.
Starter hook	Put an image of a one-parent family on the projector. Ask the students to think about the advantages and disadvantages of such an arrangement. How many of them live in a one-parent family? Ask for their experiences.
Activity One	Ask the students to go onto the Internet and research the one-parent family. There are lots of websites they can use, including Gingerbread, One Parent Family Association, One parent families and The Information Network.
Activity Two	What has caused the increase in one-parent families? Ask your students to each write their responses to this question on the whiteboard.
Activity Three	Ask your students to explore different perceptions of the one-parent family. Split them up to explore New Right perceptions, feminist assumptions, postmodern assumptions, Marxist assumptions, and so on. Encourage the students to use their 'tool kit' of theories to examine single-parent households.
Review learning	• What percentage of families are one-parent families? • Who mostly heads one-parent families? • What is the main disadvantage of one-parent families? • How does the New Right perceive one-parent families? • How do feminists view them?
Preview next lesson	Looking at gender roles in the family.
End positively	Tell the students that was the end of the largest section in this module. Tell them well done.
What the examiners are looking for	Examiners like asking why women are likely to head one-parent families, why different cultural groups are more likely to group in one-parent families, and general changes in household structure towards one-parent families.
Homework	Ask the students to find a newspaper article about one-parent families (they could search the Internet if needed). Ask them to summarise the author's views on one-parent families and to store this work in their sociology journals.
Getting the most out of your class	Take the students out to conferences. This is particularly important towards the end of the second term. It is vital to see chief examiners go through scripts, whilst interesting to listen to expert from different fields. (Examples include: http://www.a-grades.com/, http://www.philipallan.co.uk/content.aspx?page=HOME, http://www.network-training.ac.uk/)

Lesson Nine: Gender roles, domestic labour and power in the family

Topic	Group	Ability	No. of boys	No. of girls	No. of SEN	Teaching assistant
Conjugal roles.		AS				

Start positive	Tell the students it was an excellent lesson on one-parent families last time.
Connect learning	• What percentage of families are one-parent families? • Who mostly heads them? • What is the main disadvantage of one-parent families? • How does the New Right perceive one-parent families? • How do feminists view them?
Share learning objectives	• Understand the concept of conjugal roles and be able to apply this using the different types of feminism. • Understand the concept of power in the family and be able to use examples of this.
Lesson outline	An assessment of whether the symmetrical family is a fact or a myth, both in conjugal roles and decision making in the family.
Starter hook	Show three images: the pre-industrial family, the early industrial family and the symmetrical family. Ask the students to spot each example. Talk about life in each one, what the expectations of each of them are or were and what the role of children are or were, and so on.
Activity One	Ask your students to construct a questionnaire that looks at who does the housework in the family. Ask them to also include questions about other areas, such as childcare and decision-making. Ask them to give this out to their families.
Activity Two	Show the students the work of Jan Pahl. Ask your students to summarise the findings of this work, with each student picking one of the arrangements found by Pahl. Now introduce other relevant studies such as those by Ann Oakley, Edgell or Laurie and Gershuny. Ask students to analyse what these studies tell us about the nature of gender roles in the family.
Activity Three	Ask the students to interview each of their classmates to find out who makes the major decisions in their households. Ask them to compare their perceptions with the perceptions of the mother and father in each household.
Review learning	• What does symmetry mean as understood by Willmott and Young? • Give some indication that symmetry is more common now. • Which sex tends to do more housework in UK families? • What is meant by a 'double shift'? • Which sex tends to make the most important decisions in the family?
Preview next lesson	Looking at the dark side of the family.
End positively	Tell the students it was an excellent lesson on conjugal roles and power in the family.
What the examiners are looking for	Examiners tend to want to look at feminist contributions to this debate. Sometimes the focus can be related to work.
Homework	Create a family glossary, with definitions of all key concepts covered so far.
Getting the most out of your class	Ask the students to work on their journals. The students should cut out articles from the serious press and analyse them from a sociological point of view. For example, use sociological theories to make sense of the stories and to question their assumptions on everyday life.

Lesson Ten: Gender roles, domestic labour and power in the family

Topic	Group	Ability	No. of boys	No. of girls	No. of SEN	Teaching assistant
The dark side of the family.		AS				

Start positive	Tell the students that today they're going to impress you by remembering their work on 'the feminist views of the family'. Tell them you'll be looking at other problems found in families.
Connect learning	• Explain the difference between joint and segregated conjugal roles. • Which sociologists believe the modern family is symmetrical? • Name two sociologists who believe women are disadvantaged in the family. • Explain what is meant by 'dual burden'.
Share learning objectives	• Revise knowledge of the feminist views of the family. • Discuss problems that occur in families. • Assess the view that the family has a 'hidden dark side'. • Criticise this view by using existing knowledge of functionalism.
Lesson outline	Looking at the dark side of the family.
Starter hook	Ask the students to collect images of the 'cereal packet family'. Ask them to produce a collage explaining conceptions about what life is like in this family.
Activity One	Ask the students to comment on as many problems that occur in the family that they can think of. Prompt them to recall the theories of Ansley or Delphy and Leonard.
Activity Two	Start by looking at the work of Hannah Gavron and Ann Oakley. Ask the students to list the ways in which housework is alienating. Ask them to consider the links between paid employment and doing housework. Now introduce some studies that show how the family can be damaging for some of its members (relevant studies include Dobash and Dobash's study on domestic violence or Laing's radical psychiatry case study of 'Jane the tennis ball'. Remember that issues such as divorce and abuse are sensitive ones and must be handled carefully.
Activity Three	Ask the students to do some research around some of the issues that the last activity raises. Split the students and ask them to look at domestic violence, child abuse, the Child Support Agency, the consequences of divorce (particularly for children), eating disorders and mental health.
Review learning	• What is the cereal packet family? • How far does this equate to reality? • Give some evidence of the dark side of the family. • Explain the role of radical psychiatry. • How do feminists account for the dark side of the family?
Preview next lesson	Looking at childhood and how it has changed.
End positively	Tell the students it was an excellent and revealing lesson on the dark side of the family.
What the examiners are looking for	Examiners tend to look at this area of the syllabus in terms of feminism and their response to the cereal packet family.
Homework	Ask the students to write an essay: Using material from Item 1B and elsewhere assess the view that marriage remains a patriarchal institution.
Getting the most out of your class	Another way to encourage your students is to take them on educational visits. You could take them to a prison, a nursery, a court (domestic violence), and so on. Students learn far more from seeing problems in the real world, rather than just confining them to the classroom.

Lesson Eleven: The nature of childhood and changes in the status of children

Topic	Group	Ability	No. of boys	No. of girls	No. of SEN	Teaching assistant
Childhood.		AS				

Start positive	Tell the students it was a really interesting lesson last week.
Connect learning	• What is the cereal packet family? • How far does this equate to reality? • Give some evidence of the dark side of the family. • Explain the role of radical psychiatry. • How do feminists account for the dark side of the family?.
Share learning objectives	• Develop an understanding of the concept of social construction. • Understand sociological and historical evaluations of childhood. • Link sociological theory to the concept of age. • Evaluate postmodern explanations of childhood.
Lesson outline	Looking at the nature of childhood and changes in the status of children.
Starter hook	Construct a quiz based on age-related issues and ask the students to complete it. (See: http://news.bbc.co.uk/cbbcnews/hi/quiz/newsid_1855000/1855899.stm.)
Activity One	Ask the students to create a table and fill in what they would expect of people of different ages: one, 18, 40 and 70. Ask them to write what would be typical behaviour, dress, activities, where they would be allowed to go, and so on. To challenge stereotypical views of age, show a range of images, such as elderly woman riding a motorbike or young children working in third world countries. Link this to the idea of childhood as a social construction.
Activity Two	Divide an A3-sized piece of paper into appropriate dates (pre-industrial time to the present day) that catalogue the changes in childhood. So, for example, have the following headings: 'social attitudes towards children', 'who looked after the children' and 'social problems associated with childhood'. Use textbooks to obtain this information, and incorporate the work of Ariès.
Activity Three	How do we show child centeredness in modern-day society? Ask the students to list on the whiteboard. How are children protected? What experts talk about children and their needs? How are they catered for commercially? How does big business target their needs? Introduce Postman's views on the 'death of childhood'.
Review learning	• What is childhood? • What is social construction? • Explain how childhood differs between the ages. • Quote a writer who sees childhood as a social construction. • How do writers such as Neil Postman see childhood?
Preview next lesson	Looking at demography.
End positively	Tell the students you were really impressed with their knowledge today.
What the examiners are looking for	Examiners want students to be able to historically chart changes in childhood over time. Be particularly aware of the need to know changing laws, how the difference between childhood and adulthood is blurring (for example, Neil Postman).
Homework	Ask the students to use at least one website and two different textbooks to make additional notes on the following headings: 'childhood as a social construct', 'childhood in the pre-industrial era', 'factors that helped the emergence of childhood', 'childhood in the UK today' and 'childhood in the third world'. You may wish to produce a worksheet for students to fill out, and it may be worth talking about plagiarism issues to avoid copying 'word for word' from textbooks.
Getting the most out of your class	As a last exercise why not consider debating issues? This can be done via the usual debating structure (http://www.scottish.parliament.uk/vli/education/docs/enviro-studies/Debate/Duties_of_Members_of_the_Groups.pdf).

Lesson Twelve: Demographic trends in the UK since 1900

Topic	Group	Ability	No. of boys	No. of girls	No. of SEN	Teaching assistant
Demographic trends.		AS				

Start positive	Tell the students it was an excellent lesson on childhood last time.
Connect learning	• What is childhood? • What is social construction? • Explain how childhood differs between the ages. • Quote a writer who sees childhood as a social construction. • How do writers such as Neil Postman see childhood?
Share learning objectives	• Achieve an overview of demographic trends. • Understand the reasons for demographic trends. • Explain historical changes and be aware of historical chronology.
Lesson outline	Looking at birth rates, death rates and family size.
Starter hook	Using the Internet ask the students to research life expectancy in 1900 and compare with today. Ask them to look at other countries and their life expectancy rates. Which European country has the highest life expectancy?
Activity One	Conduct a card sort task in which students match the correct trends with the corresponding factors (reasons for increases and decreases in birth rates, death rates and family size). Ask your students to correctly identify if the factor quoted will increase or decrease. As a plenary exercise ask them to come up with other demographic factors that might be worth sociologists assessing.
Activity Two	Another interesting way to look at demography is to look at online census material (http://www.1901censusonline.com/. Although it will cost to download material it is not too expensive.)
Activity Three	Debate a topical issue such as fertility treatment for over 60s (http://news.bbc.co.uk/1/hi/health/4971930.stm).
Review learning	• What is happening to birth rates? • When were birth rates at their highest and lowest? • Explain the trend in mortality rates. • Explain trends in fertility.
End positively	Excellent lesson on demography in the UK.
What the examiners are looking for	As this is a new topic on the new syllabus it is perhaps important to realise why it has been added. The exam boards are keen for students to have an overview to help them contextualise sociology. You may ask why 1900? Apart from the fact that it matches the 1901 census, changes in the role of women occurred particularly at this time.
Homework	Revise the family module ready for a mock exam next lesson
Getting the most out of your class	Use of the Internet is not as easy as some students think. It is always a good idea to explain how to use search engines effectively, give appropriate web links, and show students A level specific sites such as Sociology Central: http://www.sociology.org.uk/.

Lesson One: An introduction to the role and purpose of education

Topic	Group	Ability	No. of boys	No. of girls	No. of SEN	Teaching assistant
The role and purpose of education.						

Start positive	Tell the students you will be starting with an introduction to the education system.
Connect learning	<ul><li>When was the welfare state first introduced?</li><li>Who was Beveridge?</li><li>Give one theoretical perspective on welfare.</li><li>Give a strength of this perspective.</li><li>Give a weakness of this perspective.</li></ul>
Share learning objectives	<ul><li>Determine the functions of the education system.</li><li>Demonstrate that personal experiences can be used as a basis for learning.</li><li>Engage with sociological concepts and make sociology seems real.</li></ul>
Lesson outline	An introduction to the students to the functions of the education systems and its importance to future success.
Starter hook	Ask the students to write down what they think is the purpose of the educational system.
Activity One	Working in threes, students should take turns as interviewer, interviewee and recorder. The interviewer should take a prompting role in collecting the life history of the interviewee and the recorder should note the key points. (It may be helpful to write some prompter questions on the whiteboard: experiences of good teaching, private schooling, influence of peers at school, how students have benefited from their education, and so on.) At the end of the interviewing period ask the recorder to feedback the notes, which they can discuss, clarify and amend as appropriate. When everyone has had a turn, students should examine their data looking for similarities and differences of experience and begin a tentative analysis.
Review learning	<ul><li>Give one function of the education system.</li><li>Given our autobiographies what makes a good teacher?</li><li>Name one person who has been important in your educational career.</li><li>Has race, gender or class impacted on your success?</li><li>How good were the schools you attended?</li><li>Describe the factors that were important in making a 'good' school.</li></ul>
Preview next lesson	Looking at what functionalists have to say about the role of education.
End positively	Tell the students it was an excellent lesson today.
What the examiners are looking for	Personal experience, although not admissible in an examination response, helps the pupils contextualise their education and allows them to see the factors that lead to success and failure.
Homework	Ask the students to design a poster showing how education is organised in the UK. Ask them to include nursery, primary, secondary and post-16 education (think about the different institutions that offer this), and use textbooks and the Internet to find out the usual or compulsory age ranges for each stage of education.
Getting the most out of your class	When introducing a new topic make sure that you give the students a breakdown of the different topics that are going to be covered. This allows the pupils to be aware of the chronology of the scheme of work and thereby allows them to read ahead.

Lesson Two: The role and purpose of education, including vocational education and training in contemporary society

Topic	Group	Ability	No. of boys	No. of girls	No. of SEN	Teaching assistant
The functionalist view on the role of education.						

Start positive	Tell the students it was an interesting lesson looking at their own perceptions of the education system last time.
Connect learning	• Give one function of the education system. • Given our educational autobiographies, what makes a good teacher? • Name one person who has been important in your educational career. • Has race, gender or class impacted on your success?
Share learning objectives	• Know key writers associated with functionalism. • Explain functionalist concepts. • Recognise the strengths and weaknesses of the functionalist view of education.
Lesson outline	An overview of functionalism.
Starter hook	Ask the students to suggest what norms and values are being taught in the education system. If needed, prompt them with images on projector.
Activity One	Introduce the ideas of norms and values. Show images of various social situations. Ask the students what the normal behaviour is in each circumstance. Include funerals, weddings, a court, a war zone, and so on.
Activity Two	Use the textbook or a handout to introduce the key writers (Durkheim, Parsons, Davis and Moore) and concepts of functionalism. The focus should be on the role and purpose of education (for example, as an agency for secondary socialisation and a mechanism for role allocation). Ask them to construct a concept wall. Stress the importance of key writers, key concepts, images, and strengths and weaknesses of functionalism. For each, the student should write the word with an appropriate image on some cards.
Activity Three	To integrate methods ask the students to construct a questionnaire to assess what students and parents think are the functions of education.
Review learning	• Name a writer associated with functionalism. • What are norms and values? • What does consensus mean? • Explain the phrase 'meritocracy'. • What is social solidarity? • Explain why functionalists use the organic analogy.
Preview next lesson	Looking at the conflict theory of Marxism.
End positively	Tell the students it was a good lesson on functionalist views of the educational system.
What the examiners are looking for	Examiners are keen for students to show they understand key concepts. With functionalism, questions worth two marks ask students to explain meritocracy, value consensus, role allocation, etc. Other questions on the functions of the education system are also popular.
Homework	Set the students a mini essay: Examine functionalist views on the role and purpose of education. Include some criticisms of these views (250–500 words).
Getting the most out of your class	This area of the course leads to a classic question used by the examiners, namely to evaluate what the main functions of the education system. As with other areas of the course, set regular tests to ensure your students are learning the concepts. Also use the concept wall to start and end your lesson to further help students to remember sociologists and key words.

Lesson Three: The role and purpose of education, including vocational education and training in contemporary society: Marxism

Topic	Group	Ability	No. of boys	No. of girls	No. of SEN	Teaching assistant
The Marxist view on the role of education.		AS				

Start positive	Tell the students they produced some really good work on functionalism last lesson.
Connect learning	<ul><li>Name a writer associated with functionalism.</li><li>What are norms and values?</li><li>What does consensus mean?</li><li>Explain the phrase meritocracy.</li><li>What is social solidarity?</li><li>Outline key Parsonian concepts.</li><li>Explain why functionalists use the organic analogy.</li></ul>
Share learning objectives	<ul><li>Know key writers associated with Marxism.</li><li>Explain Marxist concepts.</li><li>Recognise the strengths and weaknesses of the Marxist view of education.</li></ul>
Lesson outline	An overview of Marxist theory of education.
Starter hook	Place images of Marx, Engels and the old USSR on the overhead projector. Invite comments.
Activity One	Use the book or a handout to introduce the key writers (Marx, Bowles and Gintis, and Willis) and concepts of Marxism. The focus should be on the role and purpose of education (for example, as a tool of capitalism and a mechanism for producing docile proletariat workers). After ensuring that they understand each term ask the students to construct a concept wall. Stress the importance of key writers, key concepts, images, and strengths and weaknesses of Marxism. For each, the student should write the word with an appropriate image on some cards.
Activity Two	Produce separate cards for both definitions and key words of Marxist concepts. Include the following key terms: 'capitalism', 'bourgeoisie', 'proletariat', 'alienation', 'contradictions', 'factors of production', 'revolution', 'class consciousness', 'surplus value', 'hegemony', 'feudalism', 'the final epoch', 'superstructure' and 'infrastructure'. Ask students to match them.
Activity Three	Using a set of small cards with key Marxist and functionalist concepts, phrases and writers on them, ask the students to sort them into a functionalist pile, a Marxist pile, or a pile that can be linked to both concepts.
Review learning	<ul><li>Who are the bourgeoisie? What is the key factor that locates them within this class?</li><li>Who are the proletariat?</li><li>What do they have to do in order to survive?</li><li>What is surplus value?</li><li>What is the infrastructure?</li><li>What is the superstructure? Name some components of it.</li><li>Explain the phrase false consciousness. Give an example of it, referring to education.</li></ul>
Preview next lesson	Continue learning about Marxism, but also look at the studies by Bowles and Gintis and Willis in much more depth.
End positively	Tell the students it was a good lesson looking at Marxist explanations of the educational system.
What the examiners are looking for	Marxism is a key concept for the students and it is vital that they understand it as it provides the basis for the sociology tool kit. Examiners, of course, expect to see Marxism as an integral part of this kit.
Homework	Ask the students to create an 'education' glossary. They should include all the key functionalist and Marxist terms they have learned recently.
Getting the most out of your class	There are a number of websites that use multiple choice questions as a diagnostic tool to see if the students are understanding concepts such as Marxism. (See: http://sixthsense.osfc. ac.uk/sociology/as_sociology/marxism.asp.)

Lesson Four: The role and purpose of education, including vocational education and training in contemporary society: Marxism

Topic	Group	Ability	No. of boys	No. of girls	No. of SEN	Teaching assistant
The Marxist view on the role of education (continued).		AS				

Start positive	Tell the students it was a good lesson on the key writers and concepts of Marxism last time and now you are going to look into the studies.
Connect learning	• Who are the bourgeoisie? What is the key factor that locates them within this class? • Who are the proletariat? What do they have to do in order to survive? • What is surplus value? • What is the infrastructure? • What is the superstructure? Name some components of it. • Explain the phrase 'false consciousness'. Give an example of it.
Share learning objectives	• Be aware of the functions of the education system for Marxists. • Outline the work of Bowles and Gintis and Paul Willis. • Explain how each offers a critique of the other. • Outline the strengths and weaknesses of both pieces of research.
Lesson outline	Focussing on the studies by Willis and Bowles and Gintis.
Starter hook	Ask the students to write down what they consider are the attributes of the 'perfect student'.
Activity One	Conduct a questionnaire to assess whether the sociology students in your class are as passive and docile as Bowles and Gintis' study suggests. Are creative attributes really 'rewarded' with failure? Do students accept hierarchy? Are students really at school just to get a better job? See how far your survey backs up the work of Bowles and Gintis.
Activity Two	Construct a set of features of the hidden curriculum and then look at examples of it in your school. Think of the following: hierarchy in school, time, uniform, setting, lack of control, and so on. Can the students think of other parts of the hidden curriculum?
Activity Three	As with all theories ensure that the students can isolate strengths and weaknesses of the Marxist theory of education.
Activity Four	Contrast the work of Paul Willis. Identify a group that are anti-school in your academic institution. What behaviour did the group display? Why do the students think they behaved like this? And ultimately how did their behaviour affect them?
Review learning	• Explain the term 'hidden curriculum'. • Give an example of the hidden curriculum in action in your school. • Give one of the four ways in which the education system shapes pupils. • What is the 'correspondence principle'? Give an example.
Preview next lesson	Looking at the role and purpose of education.
End positively	Tell the students it was an interesting lesson on Bowles and Gintis and Paul Willis.
What the examiners are looking for	Examiners like students to know about how teacher and class expectations impact on performance.
Homework	Ask the students to create a presentation that compares and contrasts the functionalist and Marxist views on education. Make sure you refer to specific sociologists and their studies.
Getting the most out of your class	There are a number of videos and DVDs that can be used in sociology. Giving a commentary and asking the students to answer questions on the video helps visual learners in particular.

Lesson Five: The role and purpose of education

Topic	Group	Ability	No. of boys	No. of girls	No. of SEN	Teaching assistant
Vocational education and training, and its links to the economy.		AS				

Start positive	Tell the students they will be applying their knowledge of Marxism and functionalism to vocational education.
Connect learning	• Explain the organic analogy. • What is a meritocracy? • Describe the hidden curriculum. • How can Willis be used to criticise Bowles and Gintis?
Share learning objectives	• Explore the different types of vocational education and training in the UK. • Assess the role and prestige of these courses. • Apply sociological views.
Lesson outline	Looking at vocational courses and how they benefit the economy.
Starter hook	Write some acronyms and names of vocational courses on the whiteboard (NVQ, BTEC First, BTEC National, CACHE CCE, Key Skills, and so on). Ask the students to work out what the different letters stand for. Discuss what the different courses are and who they are aimed at.
Activity One	Distribute a range of prospectuses from local colleges and sixth forms. Ask the students to design a leaflet showing alternatives to GCSEs and A levels for 14–19-year-old students. Ask them to divide the leaflet into level two and level three courses (this may need an explanation). Prompt the students to include work-based training as well as college courses.
Activity Two	Ask students to list the benefits of vocational courses to students and employers. To extend this as a discussion, ask them if their GCSEs provided them with the skills and knowledge to survive in the workplace. Now link this to functionalism and the organic analogy, stressing the belief that vocational education clearly 'helps' the economy by producing skilled workers.
Activity Three	Test students on how much they remember on Bowles and Gintis' correspondence theory from the last lesson. Ask them to apply their theory to vocational education and training. Give prompts if needed, especially when looking at social class and the type of course chosen.
Activity Four	Hold a class debate: 'Vocational education reinforces the social class system by ensuring working-class children are trained up for working-class jobs'. Split the students into two teams: functionalists and Marxists.
Review learning	• List three vocational courses at post-16. • Why would a functionalist approve of vocational education? • What would a Marxist say about this? • Why do most upper-class students stick to 'academic' courses such as A levels?
Preview next lesson	Looking at relationships and processes in schools.
End positively	Tell the students it was a really interesting lesson today.
What the examiners are looking for	Students need to apply theoretical knowledge to current trends in the education system.
Homework	Ask the students to find a newspaper article (they could use the Internet for this) that discusses current vocational education or a specific type of course; for example, BTEC. Ask them to summarise the author's views on the value and benefits of vocational education and training. They should store the article in their sociology journal.
Getting the most out of your class	Ask the students to analyse their own reasons for studying A levels. Is their ultimate reason to get a good job?

Lesson
6

Lesson Six: Relationships and processes in schools

Topic	Group	Ability	No. of boys	No. of girls	No. of SEN	Teaching assistant
Relationships and processes in school.		AS				

Start positive	Tell the students it was an excellent lesson last time on vocational education and economy.
Connect learning	• Explain how a functionalist would link the institutions of education and the economy. • How do Bowles and Gintis explain the link between education and the workplace? • List three 'vocational' qualifications that sixth formers could study as an alternative to A levels.
Share learning objectives	• Be aware of the basic concepts of interactionism. • Link interactionism with the methodology most likely to be employed by this group of thinkers. • Quote studies that show labelling by setting and banding leading to the creation of an anti-school culture.
Lesson outline	Looking at the concept of interactionism and how it leads to the creation of an anti-school culture.
Starter hook	Ask the students to tell you when they have been labelled and what effect this has had on them.
Activity One	Make up some pen pictures of students. Perhaps you can base these on individuals that you have taught through the years. Then ask them to guess the following: their class, the kind of behaviour likely to be exhibited, how teachers would respond to the student, how the student would respond, and what would be the likely set of qualifications achieved by each student.
Activity Two	A good way to explain concepts is through diagrams. Tony Lawson's book (2000) gives a feel of how you can use diagrams. Jumble up the components that make up the self-fulfilling prophesy and ask the students to mix and match these to the correct cell. Now introduce some key studies; there are lots to choose from, including Becker, Rosenthal and Jacobsen (a good link to the use of experiments in education) and Connolly.
Activity Three	Mind maps provide another neat way of summarising information. Ask the students to work in groups to produce a mind map of the symbolic interactionist views of education, using the generic mind map in the student book as a guide.
Review learning	• What is a label? • How does this affect students? • Explain the term 'self-fulfilling prophesy'. • Name a method likely to be utilised by an interactionist sociologist. • Explain one weakness and one strength of this theoretical approach.
Preview next lesson	Looking at the interactionist perspective, but focus on sub-cultures and the curriculum.
End positively	Tell the students it was a really good lesson today.
What the examiners are looking for	Questions tend to revolve around how interaction between pupils and teachers tend to affect attainment, or how labelling is an insufficient way to explain working-class failure. Short answer questions tend to ask to explanations for self-fulfilling prophesy, streaming, and banding.
Homework	Ask the students to update their education glossary to include all the new terminology from the interactionist view of education.
Getting the most out of your class	One way to help students revise is to write out the suggested answers issued by the exam boards for all the short answer questions. You will find that some questions come up again and again. Knowing the kinds of answers that are needed helps reinforce what they need to know.

Lesson Seven: Relationships and processes in schools

Topic	Group	Ability	No. of boys	No. of girls	No. of SEN	Teaching assistant
Sub-cultures and the curriculum.		AS				

Start positive	Tell the students there were some really interesting comments raised by X last lesson.
Connect learning	• What is a label? • How does this affect students? • Explain the term 'self-fulfilling prophesy'. • Name a method likely to be utilised by an interactionist sociologist. • Explain one weakness and one strength of this theoretical approach. • What is the 'hidden curriculum'?
Share learning objectives	• Explore interactionist views on pupil sub-cultures. • Investigate sociological studies on this. • Examine links between the curriculum and the formation of sub-cultures.
Lesson outline	Looking at why pupils form sub-cultures.
Starter hook	Show images of different youth groups (emos, sports' teams, pupils behaving badly, pupils smoking, and so on). Ask students to describe how these groups would behave in school.
Activity One	Provide a clear definition of the term 'sub-culture'. Explain that interactionists are interested in how and why these are formed. Ask the students to list one study they already know about sub-cultures and use this as an opportunity to revise Willis' study. Start a discussion on whether all pupil sub-cultures are formed as a reaction against formal schooling.
Activity Two	Ask the students to work in groups to research other studies on sub-cultures using the textbook. Ensure studies covering both male and female and ethnic minority sub-cultures are included.
Activity Three	Ask each group to make a presentation on their chosen study. They should include the methods used by the sociologist, which pupils formed sub-cultures, and explain why they did this and how they acted.
Review learning	• What is a sub-culture? • Name one sociologist who has studied sub-cultures. • Describe this study. • Give three possible reasons for the formation of sub-cultures.
Preview next lesson	Looking at the links between education and social class.
End positively	Tell the students it was a good lesson on relationships and processes in schools today.
What the examiners are looking for	Sometimes essay questions in the exam are based purely on the formation of sub-cultures and how this affects attainment at school.
Homework	Ask the students to write three paragraphs explaining how the way schools are organised can result in the formation of pupil sub-cultures.
Getting the most out of your class	Provide frequent mini-tests in which students are tested on sociologists' names and the perspectives they belong to.

Lesson Eight: Differential educational achievement by social groups

Topic	Group	Ability	No. of boys	No. of girls	No. of SEN	Teaching assistant
Social class.		AS				

Start positive	Tell the students it was a great lesson on sub-cultures last time.
Connect learning	• What is a sub-culture? • Name one sociologist who has studied sub-cultures. • Describe this study. • Give three possible reasons for the formation of sub-cultures.
Share learning objectives	• Look at the links between social class and educational achievement. • Examine different sociological explanations for these. • Assess each explanation.
Lesson outline	Looking at why working-class pupils underachieve compared to middle-class pupils.
Starter hook	Initiate a game of hangman on the whiteboard. Answers could include 'restricted code', 'immediate gratification' or 'material deprivation'.
Activity One	Give an overview of the links between social class and attainment. Ask the students why they think these trends exist. Show them the league tables for GCSE results in your local area and ask them what they notice about the results of the private schools compared to state schools.
Activity Two	Create a table for each student. In the left column, write the names of key sociologists such as 'Bernstein', 'Bourdieu', 'Sugarman', 'Rist', and 'Davis and Moore'. The middle column should be left blank for students to make notes on what the theorist says about education and social class. There could also be a third column for criticisms. Help the students fill out the sections on sociologists you have already covered in previous lessons.
Activity Three	Ask the students to work in pairs to research the new sociologists using a range of texts. Alternatively, give each pair one sociologist to focus on. Answers can then be shared with the group.
Review learning	• Describe the trends for educational achievement and social class. • Explain the difference between the restricted and the elaborated codes. • What is cultural capital? • What is deferred gratification?
Preview next lesson	Looking at the links between education and gender.
End positively	Tell the students it was a good lesson looking at the links between social class and educational achievement.
What the examiners are looking for	Students may be asked to assess either internal or external explanations of working-class underachievement. It is therefore important to help students to compare and assess these explanations.
Homework	Ask the students to design a poster showing all the different theories that explain why working class pupils underachieve at school. Remember to include both internal factors (for example, labelling theory) and external factors (for example, material deprivation).
Getting the most out of your class	Carry out a 'folder inspection' each half term. Even at AS level, some students will not have the organisational ability to keep notes in order, which can cause problems when it comes to revision time!

Lesson Nine: Differential educational achievement by social groups

Topic	Group	Ability	No. of boys	No. of girls	No. of SEN	Teaching assistant
Gender: the changes in girls' achievement.		AS				

Start positive	Tell the students it was a good lesson on social class last time.
Connect learning	• Describe the trends for educational achievement and social class. • Explain the difference between the restricted and the elaborated codes. • What is cultural capital? • What is deferred gratification?
Share learning objectives	• Know contemporary trends in gender attainment in the UK. • Outline genetic and social reasons for this imbalance of attainment. • Use the 'tool box' of theories to examine reasons for differences in attainment. Notably, feminism and New Right theories of education.
Lesson outline	Looking at how and why girls were underperforming at school compared to boys before 1990.
Starter hook	Ask your students to write down as many reasons they can think of as to why girls do better than boys today.
Activity One	Ask the students to do some simple research into recent A level and GCSE examination results by gender, showing changes in achievement since the 1980s. For example, ask them to find out what percentage of boys and girls get five A*–C grades at GCSE today compared to 20 years ago. They could also get figures for their own school. Ask them to obtain similar data on A level scores, again nationally and locally. Initiate a discussion on why girls were underperforming before the 1990s.
Activity Two	Ask the students to look at one or two 'classic' studies on patriarchy in the education system (for example, Kelly's *Science for Girls* [1987]).
Activity Three	A good activity to assess the role of socialization is to get a selection of young children's books. Include some contemporary books as well as some old fashioned texts. Ask the students to comment upon the depiction of women and girls as opposed to the male characters.
Review learning	• Which sex does better at GCSE and A level today? • Why does this impact on job prospects? • Which subjects are girls and boys more likely to study at degree level? • How have female expectations changed over the last 30 years?
Preview next lesson	Focussing on why boys seem to be currently underachieving at school.
End positively	Tell the students it was a really interesting lesson on contemporary trends in gender attainment in the UK today.
What the examiners are looking for	Examiners often ask questions based on the reasons why girls' performance has improved over the last 10 years, with questions on gender regime. Essays also tend to be based on the reasons for differential performance of the genders.
Homework	Conduct an informal interview with an older, female relative or friend. Ask them to discuss their experience of school. Did they ever feel ignored by teachers? What were their aspirations at the time? What subjects did they choose to study and why?
Getting the most out of your class	As with all areas of sociology gender lends itself to using sexism within schools and outside of schools. Ask the students to name an example of top female businesspeople. How many MPs do they think are female as an overall percentage?

Lesson Ten: Differential educational achievement by social groups

Topic	Group	Ability	No. of boys	No. of girls	No. of SEN	Teaching assistant
Gender: are boys underachieving?		AS				

Start positive	Tell the students they came up with some really interesting comments about girls' achievement in exams. Tell them you're really looking forward to hearing their views on boys' achievement today.
Connect learning	• Isolate a type of feminism. • Name a writer linked to each type of fFeminism. • Give one outside school explanation for underachievement. • Give one strength of these explanations. • Give one weakness of these explanations.
Share learning objectives	• Outline reasons for male educational failure. • Assess whether this means that women will now earn the same as men in the workplace. • Question whether boys are *really* underachieving in education.
Lesson outline	Assessing why girls do so much better in examinations than boys.
Starter hook	Ask the students to write down reasons why boys do worse than girls.
Activity One	The new syllabus asks students to integrate theory and methods into the education module, so carry out some participant observation with the students. If possible, observe a single-sex science lesson. Ask the students to draw up a schedule of what they expect to see. Does reality match their expectations? If not why not?
Activity Two	Produce a set of explanations for female attainment and ask the students to evaluate each one. Student quotes are an ideal way to engender discussion on this issue. Ask the students if their school typical? Do they think that in some schools boys actually out-perform girls?
Activity Three	An effective way to improve students' written and evaluative skills is for them to see an A-grade essay. For many students using the correct structure for essays remains problematic. To teach this skill, cut up paragraphs from an A-grade essay, and then ask groups of three to reassemble it as quickly as possible. Ask the students to give it a mark out of 40: 20 marks for *knowledge and understanding* (AO1) and 20 for *interpretation, application and evaluation*. (AO2).
Review learning	• Since when has male underachievement been in issue in sociology? • Explain one reason for male underachievement. • Do you think sexism and discrimination will cease if girls continue to outperform boys in examinations? • What evidence of patriarchy is there in British society? • What reason would radical feminists give for this?
Preview next lesson	Examining the educational failure of ethnic minorities.
End positively	Tell the students it was a really good lesson today.
What the examiners are looking for	Examiners like to test students in areas such as why girls are more likely to do one subject over another, or more general questions are asked as to why girls' performance has improved so much.
Homework	Set the students a mini essay: Assess the view that the reason for the underachievement of boys is due to low teacher expectations (250–500 words). Note that students will need specific guidance on structuring this answer. Make it clear that they must compare this particular explanation of underachievement with other explanations.
Getting the most out of your class	A good way to improve student essay writing is to show them what they should aspire to. Set regular test essays, making sure you ask essay questions that you have full mark schemes for. When you have marked the full set pull out an A grade, a C grade and an E grade essay. Mark the essays with the students, and tell them exactly why the grade was obtained.

Lesson Eleven: Differential educational achievement by social groups

Topic	Group	Ability	No. of boys	No. of girls	No. of SEN	Teaching assistant
Ethnicity (outside school/external explanations).		AS				

Start positive	Tell the students it was a good lesson last time looking at why boys tend to underachieve.
Connect learning	• Since when has male underachievement been in issue in sociology? • Explain one reason for male underachievement. • Do you think sexism and discrimination will cease if girls continue to outperform boys in examinations? • What evidence of patriarchy is there in British society? • What reason would radical feminists give for this?
Share learning objectives	• Outline general trends in attainment by ethnicity. • Be aware of the different outside school explanations for varying examination performance. • Be aware of the strengths and weaknesses of outside school explanations.
Lesson outline	An assessment of the reasons why some ethnic groups do well in the British educational system, whilst some fail.
Starter hook	Ask your students to name celebrities from a range of backgrounds who come from ethnic groups other than the English, Welsh and Scottish indigenous group.
Activity One	Ask the students to research recent data on GCSE and A level results of different ethnic groups (either using textbooks or searching www.statistics.gov.uk). Which ethnic groups do best? Ask them to find reasons for this. Which groups do worst? Why might this be the case? Remember to remind them of the weaknesses of using statistics; for example, they are only one snapshot of time.
Activity Two	For the main body of the lesson ask the students to pick one of the following outside explanations for the failure of ethnic minority pupils: cultural deprivation theory, genetic differences, cultural differences, language and resistance theory. For each ask the students to research studies and then present to the class, making sure that they evaluate their theory by presenting advantages and disadvantages of each explanation. Collate the notes from each group and produce a handout for each student.
Review learning	• Which ethnic group does the best in the UK? • Which ethnic groups do poorly in comparison? • Explain genetic explanations for black attainment in school. • Explain how culture can affect ethnic attainment. • Why can language be a barrier to ethnic minority groups? • What is 'resistance theory'?
Preview next lesson	Examining inside ('internal') school explanations for ethnicity and performance in school.
End positively	Tell the students it was a really good lesson today, especially the contribution by x about y.
What the examiners are looking for	Short answer questions are very rarely asked on ethnicity beyond general questions on labelling, boys' achievement and cultural differences. However, if they are, they usually ask for sociological explanations for the underachievement of ethnic minorities.
Homework	Ask the students to design a 'revision word search', to be completed by another member of the class. Instead of listing the hidden words, ask questions. For example, 'who wrote the book *Just like a girl*?', the answer 'Sharpe' will be in your word search somewhere.
Getting the most out of your class	An excellent way to present sociological ideas whilst still encouraging creativity is by using collage. With ethnicity, explanations can be displayed pictorially encouraging ongoing learning in the classroom. There is evidence that students may benefit from sitting their external examination in their classroom, so if this is possible make sure that this happens.

Lesson Twelve: Differential educational achievement by social groups by social class, gender and ethnicity

Topic	Group	Ability	No. of boys	No. of girls	No. of SEN	Teaching assistant
Ethnicity (inside school/ internal explanations).		AS				

Start positive	Tell the students it was an excellent lesson on outside school factors, ethnicity and attainment last time.
Connect learning	• Which ethnic group does the best in the UK? • Which ethnic groups do poorly by comparison? • Why do black girls appear to do much better than their male counterparts? • Explain genetic explanations for black attainment in school. • Explain how culture can affect ethnic attainment. • Why can language be a barrier to ethnic minority groups? • What is 'resistance theory'?
Share learning objectives	• Examine whether the educational system in the UK is 'institutionally racist'. • Be aware of the main explanations for inside school failure. • Be able to distinguish between the strengths and weaknesses of each explanation.
Lesson outline	Examining inside ('internal') school explanations for ethnic underachievement.
Starter hook	Ask your students to research some facts about some different ethnic groups in the UK. Use websites such as the Equality and Human Rights Commission (www.equalityhumanrights.com/).
Activity One	Ask the students to conduct interviews with students from a variety of different ethnic backgrounds and formulate a hypothesis as to whether the education system is racist or meritocratic. Ask them to think how they can operationalise or measure factors that lead to ethnic underattainment. Ask them to use a semi-structured interview. Channel investigations to suit students' own circumstances.
Activity Two	An excellent way to examine racism is using content analysis. Before your lesson, collect a range of set texts that are used across the school. In particular find examples of texts from Geography, History, Science, Religious Education and Business Studies. Separate the students into groups and hand each of them a textbook each. Ask them to analyse it for racism and ethnocentricity.
Activity Three	Introduce studies that suggest the education system is racist, linking these to the issue of underachievement. Interesting studies include Coard, Mac an Ghaill, Sewell and Wright. Alternatively, the work of Connelly serves as both a revision of labelling and self-fulfilling prophecy theory and an explanation of why black boys underachieve.
Review learning	• How do writers such as Bernard Coard explain underachievement? • Give some evidence to suggest that schools are institutionally racist. • Why is racism difficult to measure? • Give one strength and one weakness of inside school explanations.
Preview next lesson	Looking at educational policies.
End positively	Tell the students that it was an excellent lesson on ethnicity and educational attainment.
What the examiners are looking for	Although short answer questions are rarely asked, students need to know this area of the course as full essays are often sometimes required on this topic area.
Homework	Ask the students to create a revision table showing: (a) all the internal and external explanations of ethnicity and achievement in one column, (b) an explanation of each one in the second column and (c) a criticism for each one in the third column.
Getting the most out of your class	Sociology provides an excellent opportunity for your students to learn about different cultures. Why not, for example, take them to a carnival or get a speaker in to explain them and other culturally specific events, such as New Year, Ramadan and Diwalli.

Lesson Thirteen: Educational policies

Topic	Group	Ability	No. of boys	No. of girls	No. of SEN	Teaching assistant
Historical overview		AS				

Start positive	Tell the students there were some really interesting comments about x raised by y last lesson.
Connect learning	• How do writers such as Bernard Coard explain underachievement? • Give some evidence to suggest that schools are institutionally racist. • Why is racism difficult to measure? • Give one strength and one weakness of inside school explanations.
Share learning objectives	• Explain the importance of policies and laws on educational experience and attainment. • Understand the tripartite system of the 1944 act. • Examine all parts of the 1988 act.
Lesson outline	Looking at three key educational policies.
Starter hook	Ask the students to imagine that they live in 1860. What would their lives be like? What sort of education would they receive?
Activity One	Using the student book, provide an overview of the 1870 Forster Education Act. Ask students to analyse the effect of this policy on the working classes.
Activity Two	Read aloud some typical eleven-plus test questions and ask the students to answer these in timed conditions (see, for example, www.elevenplusexams.co.uk/) Initiate a discussion on whether this is a good way to decide a pupil's secondary school. Now ask the students to make notes on the 1944 act including the tripartite system. Again, ask students to analyse the effects of this act on working class pupils. Now explain that this system mainly ended in the 1960s with the introduction of comprehensivisation, but that there are still some grammar schools today.
Activity Three	Prepare a card sort activity where students must match key components of the 1988 act (Ofsted, national curriculum, SATS, league tables, CTCs, and so on) with the correct descriptions. Answers could them be provided on a handout. Now initiate a discussion on the positive effects of this act on gender (introduction of coursework, compulsory science) compared to the less positive aspects in terms of ethnicity (ethnocentric curriculum).
Activity Four	As a plenary, ask students to log on to: http://www.educationforum.co.uk/sociology_2/historyeducation.htm and complete the gap-fill exercise.
Review learning	• Name the three key pieces of legislation. • Name three components of the 1988 act. • Explain the tripartite system. • What does 'ethnocentric' mean?
Preview next lesson	Looking at modern-day educational policies.
End positively	Tell the students that it was an interesting lesson on educational policies.
What the examiners are looking for	Students need to understand how educational policies affect the experience and attainment of different social groups, including class, ethnicity and gender.
Homework	Ask the students to create a timeline showing the dates and key content of educational policies. Pay particular attention to the 1988 Reform Act and modern-day policies.
Getting the most out of your class	www.educationforum.co.uk/sociology has a range of presentations and gap-fill exercises for revision purposes.

Lesson 14

Lesson Fourteen: Educational policies

Topic	Group	Ability	No. of boys	No. of girls	No. of SEN	Teaching assistant
Modern-day policy.		AS				

Start positive	Tell the students they did brilliant work last lesson.
Connect learning	• Name the three key pieces of legislation. • Name three components of the 1988 act. • Explain the tripartite system. • What does 'ethnocentric' mean?
Share learning objectives	• Explore the significance of parental choice and marketisation in the 1988 act. • Discuss how these are still relevant today. • Analyse other New Labour policies such as Education Maintenance Allowance (EMA).
Lesson outline	Looking at policies that affect education today.
Starter hook	To start a lively discussion about the effects of modern-day education policies, ask the class if the EMA system is fair.
Activity One	Briefly recap the main components of the 1988 act. Ensure students understand the notions of marketisation and parental choice. Using a range of texts, ask the students to make a list of the types of secondary school available today (trust, foundation, specialist, and so on). Ask them to analyse the effects of parental choice on students.
Activity Two	Introduce the policy Curriculum 2000. Link this to the wider New Labour policy of wider choice for 14–19 year olds. Ask students to research information on the new diplomas and initiate a discussion of whether this new qualification will only be taken up by 'lower ability' students.
Activity Three	As a final modern-day policy, ask students how much they expect to pay for university tuition fees. Again, ask them to analyse how top-up fees will impact on the numbers of students from working-class backgrounds applying for university places.
Review learning	• What is meant by marketisation? • How did the 1988 act encourage parental choice? • How did the New Labour government continue this policy? • How have university tuition fees affected working-class students?
Preview next lesson	Looking at the use of research methods in education.
End positively	Tell the students that it was an good lesson on how sociologists utilise methodology when studying the educational system.
What the examiners are looking for	Students need to understand how educational policies affect the experience and attainment of different social groups, including class, ethnicity and gender.
Homework	Ask the students to update their education glossary to include new terminology relating to educational policy.
Getting the most out of your class	A debate on EMA and low-income families will allow students to explore deeper issues such as the cost of education and the fairness of means-testing. This will also show links between education and the poverty modules.

Lesson Fifteen: The application of sociological research methods to the study of education

Topic	Group	Ability	No. of boys	No. of girls	No. of SEN	Teaching assistant
Research methods: experiments and social surveys.		AS				

Start positive	Tell the students it was a good lesson on modern day policy last time.
Connect learning	• What is meant by marketisation? • How did the 1988 act encourage parental choice? • How did the New Labour government continue this policy? • How have university tuition fees affected working-class students?
Share learning objectives	• Be aware of the different quantitative methods used for research within schools. • Consider the advantages and disadvantages of each of these methods. • Be able to quote examples of each method.
Lesson outline	To make students aware of the different research methods that is used within an educational setting, whilst making them aware of the advantages and disadvantages of each method.
Starter hook	Give the students a selection of research methods. For each ask them to state whether they are quantitative or qualitative. Ask them additionally to find an example of a study that uses each method.
Activity One	For the main activity ask the students to choose one research method from experiments (covering lab and field), questionnaires and structured interviews. Ask them to find out (a) examples of its use in education, (b) what the findings were of this piece of research, (c) how the researcher utilised this methodology and (d) the advantages and disadvantages of this method.
Activity Two	Ask the students to use one of the methods above and use it within a school. What did the research method involve? How easy was it to apply? Did it prove useful? Explain some strengths of the method and also explain weaknesses. Ask the students to report back to the group indicating how they got on with using their method.
Activity Three	Ask the students to pick examples of classic studies that use one methodology; for example, Rosenthal and Jacobsen's classic study on teacher expectations and the self-fulfilling prophecy. Why did they use this method? What advantages did this bring? Why could they be criticised? Is this method reliable?
Review learning	• What does the term 'quantitative' mean? • What does the term 'qualitative' mean? • Give an example of a research method linked to each of the above.
Preview next lesson	Looking at qualitative methods.
End positively	Tell the students it was a good lesson on research methods.
What the examiners are looking for	Examiners will now be asking a specific question on methods linked to education. Exemplars indicate that students will need to be able to assess the strengths and limitations of a variety of methods. These include interviews, questionnaires, official statistics and observation.
Homework	Set the students a mini-essay: Assess the usefulness of questionnaires in education research.
Getting the most out of your class	Whilst there will be no coursework in the new specification, this does not preclude setting mini projects for your students to attempt. Why not use titles successfully used in previous A2 or AS coursework?

Lesson Sixteen: The application of sociological research methods to the study of education

Topic	Group	Ability	No. of boys	No. of girls	No. of SEN	Teaching assistant
Research methods: interviews and observation.		AS				

Start positive	Tell the students it was a good lesson on research methods last time.
Connect learning	<ul><li>What is quantitative data?</li><li>List three quantitative methods used when studying education.</li><li>Give one advantage of using questionnaires when studying education.</li><li>State two problems of using a lab experiment to study education.</li><li>Suggest one education study that used a field experiment.</li></ul>
Share learning objectives	<ul><li>To be aware of the different qualitative methods used for research within schools.</li><li>Consider the advantages and disadvantages of each of these methods.</li><li>Be able to quote examples of each method.</li></ul>
Lesson outline	To make students aware of the different research methods that is used within an educational setting, whilst making them aware of the advantages and disadvantages of each method.
Starter hook	Present students with a card sort activity that matches the sociologist to the research method used.
Activity One	Ask the students to choose one research method from unstructured interviews, participant observation and non-participant observation. Ask them to find out (a) examples of its use in education, (b) what the findings of this piece of research were, (c) how the researcher utilised this methodology and (d) the advantages and disadvantages of this method.
Activity Two	Ask the students to use one of the methods above and use it within a school. What did the research method involve? How easy was it to apply? Did it prove useful? Explain some strengths of the method and also explain weaknesses. Ask the students to report back to the group, indicating how they got on with using their method.
Activity Three	Another way to do this is to ask the students to pick examples of classic studies that use one methodology; for example, Paul Willis' participant observation method utilised in *Learning to Labour* (1977). Why did he use this method? What advantages did this bring? Why could he be criticised? Is this method reliable?
Review learning	<ul><li>What does the term 'quantitative' mean?</li><li>What does the term 'qualitative' mean?</li><li>Give an example of a research method linked to each of the above.</li></ul>
Preview next lesson	Looking at the use of secondary data.
End positively	Tell the students that it was an illuminating lesson looking at how different methods have been used by various educational researchers.
What the examiners are looking for	Examiners will now be asking a specific question on methods linked to education. Exemplars indicate that students will need to be able to assess the strengths and limitations of a variety of methods. These include interviews, questionnaires, official statistics and observation.
Homework	Ask the students to produce a presentation that assesses the usefulness of either unstructured interviews or participant observation in education research.
Getting the most out of your class	Whilst there will be no coursework in the new specification, this does not preclude setting mini projects for your students to attempt. Why not use titles successfully used in previous A2 or AS coursework?

Lesson Seventeen: The application of sociological research methods to the study of education

Topic	Group	Ability	No. of boys	No. of girls	No. of SEN	Teaching assistant
Secondary data.		AS				

Start positive	Tell the students it was a good lesson on research methods last time.
Connect learning	• What does the term 'quantitative' mean? • What does the term 'qualitative' mean? • Give an example of a research method linked to each of the above. • Give an example of how each method has been used in education research.
Share learning objectives	• Distinguish between primary and secondary data. • List the types of secondary data used by sociologists. • Examine the use of official statistics and other documents in education research.
Lesson outline	Looking at how sociologists make use of secondary data when conducting education research.
Starter hook	Give each student a sticky note with a research method written on it. Write two headings on the whiteboard: 'primary' and 'secondary'. Ask the students to place their sticky note under the correct heading.
Activity One	If not already covered in another module, give the students clear definitions of primary and secondary data. Ask them to think of examples of secondary data that can be used to study education.
Activity Two	Introduce the use of official statistics in education by showing the students copies of league tables. Ask them to discuss the usefulness of these from both a Marxist and an interactionist approach.
Activity Three	Show students the Ofsted website. If appropriate, download the latest inspection for your school or college and link this to the use of public documents in education research.
Activity Four	Ask the students to make notes on the study by Valerie Hey (2003), concentrating on her use of life documents (notes passed in class) to understand friendship in schools. Again, start a discussion on the usefulness of this king of secondary source.
Review learning	• Explain what is meant by primary and secondary data. • How can official statistics prove useful when studying education? • How can public documents prove useful? • What problems are associated with using secondary data in education research?
End positively	Tell the students that was an interesting lesson on statistics relating to the educational system.
What the examiners are looking for	Examiners will now be asking a specific question on methods linked to education. Exemplars indicate that students will need to be able to assess the strengths and limitations of a variety of methods. These include, interviews, questionnaires, official statistics, observation, and so on.
Homework	Ask the students to revise this module in preparation for a mock exam next lesson.
Getting the most out of your class	Ask the students to look at the mind maps in the student textbook and make their own improved versions. Highlight the helpfulness of using different colours and symbols.

Health and illness

Lesson One: Health, illness, disability and the body as social and biological constructs

Topic	Group	Ability	No. of boys	No. of girls	No. of SEN	Teaching assistant
Introduction: key concepts and definitions.		AS				
Start positive	Tell the students that they are moving onto a new area of sociology: health.					
Connect learning	• What does the term 'quantitative' mean? • What does the term 'qualitative' mean? • Give an example of a research method linked to each of the above.					
Share learning objectives	• Understand differing definitions of health, illness and disability.					
Lesson outline	An assessment of the definitions of health and illness, with reference to the biomedical model and complementary medicine.					
Starter hook	Ask the students to define health. What are the characteristics of a healthy person? Ask them to compare their ideas of what being healthy are with their classmates.					
Activity One	Ask the students to compare their definitions of health to the World Health Organisation definition (see: http://www.who.int/about/definition/en/print.html). Next ask the students to define illness. Ask them to write out a selection of statements that operationalise the concept of illness. Which conditions are easy to define as illnesses? Which are much more difficult to define? Introduce the notion that health and illness can be considered social constructions.					
Activity Two	Ask the students to define disability. Ask them to compare their definitions to the official definition of disability as stated in the Disability Discrimination Act (see: http://www.direct.gov.uk/en/DisabledPeople/RightsAndObligations/DisabilityRights/DG_4001069).					
Activity Three	Ask the students to split up into small groups. Ask half to research the medical model of health and produce a summary of its suggestions. Ask them to address how the model defines health, illness and disability. Ask the other groups to research the social model of health, including its views on alternative complementary therapies. How does the model define health, illness and disability? When finished, each group researching the social model of health should join a group researching the biomedical model to share and explain ideas.					
Activity Four	Use textbooks or handouts to cover definitions of the body. Initiate this by asking students to describe the 'perfect' male and female bodies. Discuss how our notions of perfection derive from the media. Link back to the notion of social construct.					
Review learning	• Define the term 'health'. • Define the term 'illness'. • Define the term 'disability'. • Why are these difficult to define? • What is complementary medicine?					
Preview next lesson	Looking at the biomedical model in much more depth next lesson.					
End positively	Tell the students it was a really good start to the module.					
What the examiners are looking for	Examiners like to link definitions to concepts such as social construction.					
Homework	Ask the students to start a health glossary and include the new concepts learned today.					
Getting the most out of your class	Why not consider asking your local GP to talk to your class about health in your locality?					

Lesson Two: Health, illness, disability and the body as social and biological constructs

Topic	Group	Ability	No. of boys	No. of girls	No. of SEN	Teaching assistant
The biomedical model of health.		AS				

Start positive	Tell the students it was a good lesson last time looking at how sociologists and laypeople define health, illness and disability.
Connect learning	<ul><li>Define the term 'health'.</li><li>Define the term 'illness'.</li><li>Define the term 'disability'.</li><li>Why are these difficult to define?</li><li>What is complementary medicine?</li><li>Why it is not universally accepted by the NHS?</li></ul>
Share learning objectives	<ul><li>Understand the medical model's view of illness.</li><li>Criticise this model.</li></ul>
Lesson outline	Looking at the biomedical model of health and assess it in relation to time, culture and alternative therapies.
Starter hook	Place medical images (doctors, hospitals, and so on) on the overhead projector and ask the students to write down words that they associate with these images. Explore how the medical model is linked with their appearance and their status.
Activity One	Ask the students to produce a timeline displaying the major medical breakthroughs since the mid-nineteenth century. Ask students to produce different timelines using different models. Ask them to contrast a timeline using the biomedical model with the complementary (social) model (they will have to start their timeline far earlier for this model). By using this method your students will be able to see the different focus used by each system. This could be extended by looking at different cultures such as Chinese medicine.
Activity Two	Ask the students to choose a particular condition and explain how the medical model has 'medicalised' it. Ask them to choose from the following list: disability, pregnancy, childbirth, depression, female sexual dysfunction, obesity and death. Perhaps ask the students to produce a mobile, presentation, a poster, and so on.
Review learning	<ul><li>How is illness caused according to the medical model?</li><li>Describe how the model suggests it should be treated.</li><li>How are medical professionals portrayed in this model?</li><li>Give one criticism of the medical model.</li></ul>
Preview next lesson	The next lesson will examine social class and health inequalities.
End positively	Tell the students it was another great lesson.
What the examiners are looking for	Examiners often ask for components of the biomedical model, so students will need to know that it is curative, hospital-based, scientific and rational.
Homework	Ask the students to create a poster that compares the social and medical models of health. Remember to include problems with each model.
Getting the most out of your class	Visits are a good way to engage pupils. Why not take your pupils to a visit to a health centre, hospital or doctor's surgery?

Lesson Three: The unequal social distribution of health and illness by social groups

Topic	Group	Ability	No. of boys	No. of girls	No. of SEN	Teaching assistant
Social class and health.		AS				

Start positive	Tell the students you really liked their presentations on x last lesson.
Connect learning	• How is illness caused according to the medical model? • Describe how the model suggests it should be treated. • How are medical professionals portrayed in this model? • Give one criticism of the medical model.
Share learning objectives	• Outline general trends in relation to social class and mortality and morbidity. • Assess differing explanations for this and use examples to explain these.
Lesson outline	An assessment of the links between social class and mortality and morbidity.
Starter hook	Ask your students to research how many different classification systems there are for social class. (Link back to the lesson plan on poverty and social groups from Topic One). How are they similar? What are the main differences between the systems? Ask the students to then classify a few occupations using both criteria.
Activity One	Ask the students to do some research on the general trends on the link between social class and morbidity and then present these findings back to the class. Split them into groups which require them to look at different statistical sources, such as the *General Household Survey* (http://www.statistics.gov.uk/ssd/surveys/general_household_survey.asp), *the Black Report* (http://www.scotpho.org.uk/nmsruntime/saveasdialog.asp?lID = 1057&sID = 1655) and *Health inequalities and New Labour* (http://www.bmj.com/cgi/content/full/330/7498/1016).
Activity Two	Introduce the two main explanations of why the working classes are most likely to suffer from poor health (cultural and structural). Compare these to other explanations such as the artefact approach and the theory of social selection. Then ask the students to pick one of the approaches to explain the differences in health between the social classes. For each ask them to consider various factors. With social selection, how do people move up and down the class system? And how does health affect this movement? What strengths can they isolate for each? Conversely what criticisms can be levelled at each explanation?
Activity Three	For the cultural explanation ask the students to think of the poor health habits exhibited by the lower social classes. How does this contrast with the middle classes? Particularly ask them to concentrate on smoking, drinking, diet, exercise, and so on. Ask the students to research the most dangerous jobs. Why are they so dangerous?
Review learning	• Give one way that is used to measure social class. • Explain the link between social class and health. • Outline one explanation for this link. • Give one strength and one weakness of this explanation.
Preview next lesson	Examining how health varies between gender.
End positively	Tell the students there were some complex theories covered today. Tell them well done.
What the examiners are looking for	Examiners like to use short answer questions about class factors that lead to illness. Essays tend to go for an overall approach to differences in health between all factors including social class, or go for looking at a specific cause of social inequality expecting other social class factors to also be included.
Homework	Ask the students to find a newspaper article that covers health and social class (for example, binge drinking, breastfeeding, and so on). Ask them to write a short review, deciding whether the author is offering an explanation of the links and to store this work in their sociology journals.
Getting the most out of your class	*Sociology Review* (Philip Allen Publishers) publishes articles that, although tending to be written with higher ability students in mind, can be made more accessible. For example, the article *Unequal Unhealthy Nation* (1999) provides a useful starting point for health inequalities in the UK.

Lesson Four: The unequal social distribution of health and illness by social groups

Topic	Group	Ability	No. of boys	No. of girls	No. of SEN	Teaching assistant
Gender and health.		AS				

Start positive	Tell the students that the last lesson was really productive.
Connect learning	• Clarify a method used to measure social class. • Explain the link between social class and health. • Outline one explanation for this link. • Give one strength and one weakness of this explanation.
Share learning objectives	• Understand the relationship between gender and mortality and morbidity. • Be aware and understand different explanations for the above.
Lesson outline	Comparing patterns of illness for women and men in contemporary British society.
Starter hook	Read aloud some 'facts' on gender and health and ask the students to decide if each fact is true or false (see: http://www.genderandhealth.ca/en/modules/depression/depression-impact-and-incidence-04.jsp).
Activity One	Using the *General Household Survey,* ask your students to obtain data on gender and health. For example, longevity, which gender visits the doctor most, the differences between male and female diseases and mental health.
Activity Two	Introduce theories that explain gender differences in health (biological differences, socialisation, increased awareness, sexism from doctors, and so on). Produce a set of prompt cards with key words that relate to genetic, cultural, material and unequal treatment of women by the NHS. Ask the students to sort them by explanation and then summarise them in a paragraph explaining each approach.
Activity Three	Initiate a discussion on how men and women perceive health differently (this could lead to a good-humoured debate on issues such as 'man flu'!) Ask the students to get into groups to prepare a questionnaire to operationalise the differences between the sexes. For example, how often they have been off work, the illnesses they have suffered, how they see their health on that day, and so on. Ask each group to present their findings back to the class as a whole.
Review learning	• Isolate one difference between the genders when it comes to health. • Clarify how the genetic and biological approach explains these differences. • Give one indication of how women's health suffers because of their behaviour. • Explain how material factors influence the health of women.
Preview next lesson	Next lesson we will be looking at differences in health between ethnic groups.
End positively	Tell the students there were some really good discussion points raised today.
What the examiners are looking for	Questions crop up in both short answer and essay format on explaining differences in health chances between the genders, why women outlive men or why women visit the doctor more often than men.
Homework	Set the students a mini-essay: Assess the materialist explanation of class inequalities in health (300–500 words).
Getting the most out of your class	With the new course there should be more time to indulge your students in topic work. Students could examine particular issues such as why women smoke more than men, how the workplace affects women's health, if women are treated equally within the health service. With health, there are opportunities to visit hospitals, doctor surgeries, and so on.

Lesson Five: The unequal social distribution of health and illness by social groups

Topic	Group	Ability	No. of boys	No. of girls	No. of SEN	Teaching assistant
Ethnicity and health.		AS				

Start positive	Tell the students you've enjoyed marking their homework. Tell them there were some really good pieces of work.
Connect learning	• Isolate one difference between the genders when it comes to health. • Clarify how the genetic and biological approach explains these differences. • Give one indication of how women's health suffers because of their behaviour. • Explain how material factors influence the health of women.
Share learning objectives	• Discover trends about the health of different ethnic groups. • Assess explanations for these differences. • Evaluate the strengths and weaknesses of each of these explanations.
Lesson outline	An assessment of the health of ethnic groups in the UK and why some groups are more likely to suffer from illness.
Starter hook	Ask the students to search the percentage make-up of ethnic groups in Britain.
Activity One	Ask the students to log onto the following website: http://www.raceequalityfoundation. org.uk/hsc/files/health-brief6.pdf. Ask them to summarise the patterns of morbidity and mortality for various ethnic groups. What data is available? Why was there so little work done in this area before 1991?
Activity Two	Introduce the main debate when looking at the explanations for the inequalities. Are cultural or material factors to blame? If handled sensitively, this could lead to a valuable discussion on issues such as racism in the NHS, or the higher incidence of depression and unemployment among African-Caribbean men in the UK.
Activity Three	Tables are an excellent way of summarising information for sociology students. Ask them to construct a table to précis explanations of different morbidity and mortality between ethnic groups. Cells should include explanation, writers, strengths and weaknesses. You could use large A3 grids, which have already been created in a word processor with the appropriate cells. It is important that students research this information either through their notes or the Internet. It is always a good idea, however, to have an answer grid available to help those who find such a task difficult.
Review learning	• Give one genetic illness that affects an ethnic group. • Isolate how the behaviour of ethnic minority groups may impact on their health. • Clarify how material factors can impact on the health of ethnic minority groups. • How does racism affect health?
Preview next lesson	Examining how provision differs for the different social groups in society.
End positively	Tell the students it was a really good lesson today.
What the examiners are looking for	Short answer questions can ask about access to the health care system, or general essay questions on examining the reasons why ethnic groups experience poorer health than the rest of the population. Or students can be asked about health chances and health care differences for ethnic groups.
Homework	Ask the students to write three paragraphs outlining the reasons why some ethnic groups have worse health than others.
Getting the most out of your class	Teachers need to be aware of different ethnic groups in their class. A good way to avoid conflict is to ask questions around the class in the same order, so everyone gets exactly the same share of questions.

Lesson Six: The unequal social distribution of health and illness by social groups

Topic	Group	Ability	No. of boys	No. of girls	No. of SEN	Teaching assistant
Region and health.		AS				

Start positive	Tell the students it was an excellent lesson on ethnicity last time.
Connect learning	• Give one genetic illness that affects an ethnic group. • Isolate how the behaviour of ethnic minority groups may impact on their health. • Clarify how material factors can impact on the health of ethnic minority groups. • How does racism affect health?
Share learning objectives	• Discover trends about the health of rural and urban areas. • Assess explanations for these differences. • Explain the implications of the postcode lottery.
Lesson outline	Looking at health in different regions.
Starter hook	Give each student a mock postcode written on a card. Have small prizes (pencils, sweets, and so on) ready. To demonstrate the postcode lottery, call out postcodes. For example, "Everyone with a BM postcode wins a sweet, anyone with an EX postcode wins nothing!"
Activity One	Provide students with a clear definition of the postcode lottery. Initiate a discussion on the fairness of this.
Activity Two	Give each student a copy of an article on the postcode lottery (for example, http://www.guardian.co.uk/society/2000/nov/09/NHS). Ask the students to work in pairs to come up with a clear explanation of the inverse care law.
Activity Three	Introduce health differences in urban and rural areas. Topics to cover could include pollution, life expectancy, infant mortality rates and availability of services. Students should use a range of textbooks to find statistics on these topics.
Review learning	• List three social factors that could affect health • What is the postcode lottery? • What is the inverse care law? • Explain the key health differences between urban and rural areas.
Preview next lesson	Examining how provision differs for the different social groups in society.
End positively	Tell the students it was a really good lesson today.
What the examiners are looking for	Students should be able to link all of the factors affecting health. For example, people living in large cities are also likely to be working class or ethnic minorities.
Homework	Ask the students to find another article on the postcode lottery. Ask them to write a brief summary of the article in their sociology journals.
Getting the most out of your class	Encourage students to subscribe to magazines that will enhance their learning. SureStart and OZONE magazines are free of charge.

Lesson Seven: Inequalities in health care

Topic	Group	Ability	No. of boys	No. of girls	No. of SEN	Teaching assistant
Inequalities in health provision.		AS				

Start positive	Tell the students it was a good lesson last time on region and health.
Connect learning	• Give one genetic illness that affects an ethnic group. • Isolate how the behaviour of ethnic minority groups may impact on their health. • Clarify how material factors can impact on the health of ethnic minority groups. • How does racism affect health?
Share learning objectives	• Contextualise the current position of the NHS. • Explain factors that influence the provision of, and access to, health care provision in the UK. • Clarify how different groups are treated by the system. • Understand how theoretical perspectives would explain these differences. • Evaluate each of these explanations being aware of their strengths and weaknesses.
Lesson outline	An evaluation of the provision of health care to various groups within the UK.
Starter hook	Ask the students to look on the Internet to answer the question 'How many health services around the world are state funded? Ask them to produce a European map to exemplify the current situation.
Activity One	As a general starter to health service provision in the UK ask the students to produce an image line to show the key dates that explain how health service provision has changed since 1945. Ask them to get appropriate images off the Internet and collate them into their timelines.
Activity Two	Ask the students to draw mind maps or spider diagrams to explain how access to health care varies between different groups. For social classes, for example, they should place factors such as income, locality, car ownership and working hours into their diagrams. Students should draw on work covered in previous lessons to encompass class, gender and ethnicity, and remember to include age too. Ask the students to exemplify each and to use appropriate studies that back their arguments. Ensure that images remain a central component of the diagram, encouraging both visual and verbal learners to benefit from this activity.
Activity Three	Ask the students to produce posters or presentations that compare the NHS to the private healthcare sector in the UK. Use data (for example, www.nhs.uk and www.bupa.co.uk) to compare the differences between the two in terms of cost, provision, life expectancy, comfort, and so on. As a valuable revision activity, link this into a discussion on the postcode lottery covered last lesson: people living in an area where their desired treatment is not available on the NHS may be more likely to go private.
Review learning	• Isolate an important date for the NHS in Britain. • How does geography impact on provision? • Explain the influence of the medical profession on provision. • How does provision change by gender, social class and ethnicity? • Give one theoretical response to why this is the case.
Preview next lesson	The next lesson will examine mental illness in contemporary British society.
End positively	Tell the students there were some really interesting comments made today.
What the examiners are looking for	Examiners like to ask questions on the health care chances and differences in health care for ethnic minority groups or why ethnic groups suffer from poorer health in general.
Homework	Ask the students to update their health glossaries to include all the new concepts learned in recent lessons.
Getting the most out of your class	Why not type out the 40 mark questions for January and June exams and examine the patterns that occur? You can usually find out which questions are asked regularly and discuss these with the students. Equally, more marginal areas often appear on a regular basis.

Lesson Eight: The sociological study of mental illness

Topic	Group	Ability	No. of boys	No. of girls	No. of SEN	Teaching assistant
Introduction and key concepts.		AS				

Start positive	Tell the students it was an excellent lesson on health inequalities last time.
Connect learning	• Isolate an important date for the NHS in Britain. • How does geography impact on provision? • Explain the influence of the medical profession on provision. • How does provision change by gender, social class and ethnicity? • Give one theoretical response to why this is the case.
Share learning objectives	• Clarify the problems of defining 'mental illness'. • Look at the causes of mental illnesses.
Lesson outline	An assessment of what mental illness is and who suffers the most from the condition.
Starter hook	Discuss what mental illness is with the students. Give them some examples.
Activity One	Ask the students to construct a survey to operationalize mental illness. Ask the students to come up with a list of behaviours and then conduct their surveys, asking the respondents to tick off how far that behaviour is considered abnormal or normal. Which behaviours were most abnormal? Why was this considered to be the case? Was the deviant behaviour due to mental illness?
Activity Two	On an overhead projector, show two columns of information. On the left, have a list of key terms related to mental health (some of which will be familiar to students if you have already taught other modules such as *education*). Include norms, deviance, social construct, labelling, depression and possibly some more specific terms such as schizophrenia, multiple personality disorder, and so on. In the right column are the corresponding definitions, but in the wrong order. Students must 'pair up' the correct definitions and add them to their health glossary.
Activity Three	Introduce a brief history of mental illness. Include alternative cures such as exorcism (see: http://www.guardian.co.uk/society/2001/may/02/socialcare.mentalhealth1 for an interesting article on how the Christian Church uses exorcism for suspected mental illness). Now introduce the social groups that are most likely to be diagnosed with mental illness (women, the working classes, the elderly and African-Caribbean men). Ask the students to research on the Internet how ethnicity and mental illness are linked. Ask them to find out why there is little research available, how unequal treatment of ethnic groups occurs, evidence of racism in the health service and which mental illnesses are most likely to be suffered by each ethnic group. Finally make some recommendations on how the treatment of all ethnic groups could be improved.
Review learning	• Why is it difficult to measure mental illness? • Give one example of how mental illness has been treated. • What is the link between mental health and ethnicity? • What is the link between mental health and gender?
Preview next lesson	Looking at mental health and labelling.
End positively	Tell the students that there were some excellent observations about the problems of measuring mental illness.
What the examiners are looking for	Essay questions on labelling are often asked, along with similar notions of social construction and definition.
Homework	Set and appropriate essay on mental illness. (See www.aqa.org.uk for some examples.)
Getting the most out of your class	An important part of promoting sociology as a subject is making sure that your students have access to excellent resources. Make sure that students go to the library and befriend their librarian. Having an excellent relationship with them allows you to increase both set texts and journals within the school library. Given how literate a subject sociology is, it is vital that students are encouraged to visit and the library and read journals, magazines and books that promote their knowledge base.

Lesson Nine: The sociological study of mental illness

Topic	Group	Ability	No. of boys	No. of girls	No. of SEN	Teaching assistant
Mental health: a real problem or a social construction?		AS				

Start positive	Tell the students you're going to continue from the good lesson last week.
Connect learning	• Why is it difficult to measure mental illness? • Give an example of how mental illness has been treated. • What is the link between mental health and ethnicity? • What is the link between mental health and gender?
Share learning objectives	• Apply interactionist theory to the study of mental health. • Look at studies on mental health by Rosenhan Goffman and Foucault.
Lesson outline	Looking at whether mental health is just a social construction.
Starter hook	Read the following aloud to the students and let them think of answers: 'A well-educated man repeatedly refuses to shake his doctor's hand. He seems withdrawn, not speaking at all. He is eventually diagnosed with a mental illness, but could there be another explanation for his behaviour?'
Activity One	Explain that the man was deeply religious and had taken a vow of silence. He refused to shake his female doctor's hand because his religion states that he must not physically touch a stranger of the opposite sex. Now link this to the idea of mental illness as a social construction.
Activity Two	Introduce labelling theory and the self-fulfilling prophecy. Ask students how this can be applied to mental health. Link this to Rosenhan and Goffman's study, asking students to make notes using the textbook.
Activity Three	Now introduce Foucault's work on 'madness' as irrationality. Again, explain to the class that it is those in power (medical professionals) who get to decide what is a 'mental illness' and what is 'sane'.
Activity Four	Start a class debate: interactionists versus. realists. Students must quote statistics and studies to decide whether or not mental health is a social construction.
Review learning	• Why is it difficult to measure mental illness? • Explain how Foucault sees mental illness and its definition. • What is meant by a self-fulfilling prophecy? • Give one argument to suggest that mental illness is a real problem.
Preview next lesson	Looking at how the media stigmatises mental patients and how this might affect them.
End positively	Tell the students that an interesting debate resulted from looking at how mental health is socially constructed.
What the examiners are looking for	Essay questions on labelling are often asked, along with similar notions of social construction and definition.
Homework	Ask the students to design a revision poster showing the key sociologists, studies and concepts for mental health.
Getting the most out of your class	In debates, select the more confident students to be 'team leaders'. Their job is to ensure that all their team members are included in the debate. This ensures that the loudest students do not dominate the discussion.

Lesson Ten: Mental health interactionism and stigma

Topic	Group	Ability	No. of boys	No. of girls	No. of SEN	Teaching assistant
The sociological study of the nature and social distribution of mental illness.		AS				

Start positive	Tell the students it was an excellent lesson on introducing mental health last time.
Connect learning	• Why is it difficult to measure mental illness? • Explain how Foucault sees mental illness and its definition. • Clarify the reasons why women are more prone to mental illness than men. • Describe why ethnic minority groups tend to suffer more from mental illness than other groups.
Share learning objectives	• Examine the different groups that are stigmatised by the press and medical profession. • Isolate the effect of this on the group concerned. • Clarify how interactionism can be evaluated.
Lesson outline	An assessment of the stereotyping process as it relates to mental health.
Starter hook	Construct flash cards with legal and illegal activities written on them. Ask the students to examine whether the behaviour on the card was ever legal.
Activity One	Ask the students to pick one of the following conditions: AIDS, schizophrenia, anorexia nervosa, obsessive compulsive disorder and bipolar disorder. With each condition, ask the group to investigate how they have been stigmatized. Investigate the media to find out the phrases that are used to report such illnesses (violent? threat? danger?). What impact does such coverage have? It is fair, rational? Or is it a way of stigmatising the group from the rest of society.
Activity Two	From a similar standpoint, ask the students to construct mobiles with press cuttings on how each of the above illnesses is covered by the mass media. When this content analysis has been performed use interactionist analysis to explain the impact and affect on the groups concerned. Use other theoretical perspectives to criticise this view. Make sure students use different card and colour-coded areas to clearly delineate the differing arguments offered by the mobile.
Review learning	• How do interactionists like to do their research? • Explain the advantages of this method. • How can stereotyping be criticised? • Name a mental illness. • Give an example of how this group is viewed by the mass media and or doctors.
Preview next lesson	Looking at the role of health professionals.
End positively	Tell the students very interesting information was found during their research.
What the examiners are looking for	Essay questions focus on different social groups and mental illness and short questions ask for students to be targeted on gender and why women suffer more from mental illness.
Homework	Ask the students to design a presentation that compares the medical explanation of mental illness to the interactionist explanation. They should include concepts such as labelling, stigma and include the role of the media.
Getting the most out of your class	Mental illness is an area that has been explored in films. An excellent way to introduce the subject of mental illness is by showing the film *One Flew Over the Cuckoo's Nest* (1975). How is McMurphy evaluated? Why has McMurphy been admitted? How does McMurphy rebel against the sadistic Nurse Ratched? With all videos ensure that your students have ready-prepared questions to answer, rather than being left to passively watch the film. Stop at salient points and point out the relationship between the film and the sociology of mental health.

Lesson Eleven: The role of health professionals

Topic	Group	Ability	No. of boys	No. of girls	No. of SEN	Teaching assistant
The role of medicine and health professionals.		AS				

Start positive	Tell the students it was an excellent lesson on mental health last time.
Connect learning	• How do interactionists like to do their research? • Explain the advantages of this method. • How can stereotyping be criticised? • Name a mental illness • Give an example of how this group is viewed by the mass media and doctors.
Share learning objectives	• Discover how the medical profession is changing since the post 2004 reforms in the NHS. • Understand how doctors and nurses view their roles. • Assess how different theoretical perspectives view the medical profession.
Lesson outline	An assessment of the duties and esteem of medical professionals in the UK.
Starter hook	Divide the students into two teams. One person from each team should sit at the front, facing away from the whiteboard. Now write a name of a perspective, key functionalist or Marxist on the board. The teams should describe the word to the person at the front. The first person to guess the word wins a point for their team. This game serves as a useful recap of sociological perspectives, which may not have been visited for awhile.
Activity One	Give each student a particular perspective to look at and ask them to research how that perspective perceives the medical profession. Again use Marxism, Weberian, feminism, functionalism and Foucault as the theories. You may wish to provide worksheets with specific questions depending on the perspective; for example, students researching feminism could be directed to look at Oakley's *From here to Maternity* (1979) study, whilst the Marxist worksheet could contain questions on private health companies, and the NHS worksheet as a way to ensure the workforce remains able to work.
Activity Two	A topical area in which to do some research on is how the role of doctors and nurses in changing in the NHS. Arrange a visit to a local hospital. Interview both nurses and doctors as to how the changes have affected their roles. If this is not possible, use the Internet to produce a presentation showing how the nursing profession is being 'professionalised'.
Activity Three	Using the Internet (for example, the General Medical Council website), ask the students to research a day in the life of different types of doctors. Look at the following specialists: GPs, surgeons, specialists and complementary doctors. For each ask them to find the following detail: what their day consists of, what their wage is, how much they earn outside of the NHS and how the new NHS contract post 2004 has impacted on them. If this detail is difficult to find out, why not email your local primary care trust or invite an accommodating local GP to talk about their job?
Review learning	• Explain how nursing is being professionalised. • Name the organisations that govern the medical profession. • How have changes in the NHS contract impacted on the profession? • Isolate how Marxism, feminism, Weberian, functionalist and Foucault would see the role of the medical profession.
Preview next lesson	Looking at methods that are used to examine health.
End positively	Tell the students it's great to see how enthusiastic they've been today.
What the examiners are looking for	Essay questions ask how and why doctors receive such a high status, or how effective medicine and medical professionals are in 'curing' ill health.
Homework	Ask the students to use at least two different textbooks to find studies on the sociology of health that have used experiments, observation, interviews, questionnaires and official statistics.
Getting the most out of your class	Rather than always setting rigid homework that ask students to write essays, occasionally ask them to find out detail that embellishes their sociological knowledge and allows them to use 'sociological insight'.

Lesson Twelve: Integrating theory and methods

Topic	Group	Ability	No. of boys	No. of girls	No. of SEN	Teaching assistant
The application of sociological research methods to the study of health.		AS				

Start positive	Tell the students it was an excellent lesson on perspectives on health last time.
Connect learning	• How do interactionists like to do their research? • Explain the advantages of this method. • How can stereotyping be criticised? • Name a mental illness. • Give an example of how this group is viewed by the mass media and or doctors.
Share learning objectives	• Use methods and theory in context. • Put these into concrete action. • Evaluate sociological theory.
Lesson outline	The application of social research to the study of health.
Starter hook	Mix and match examples of research and writers onto flash cards and ask the students to match the appropriate writer to the appropriate important study.
Activity One	Ask the students to pick a method of social research from the last topic within the textbook. Allocate the following: surveys, interviews, life histories, participant observation, non-participant observation, experiments and secondary data. Ask them to conduct sociological research into one area of health using the method they have been given. Possible areas could include health in the locality, eating disorders, the quality of the local primary care trust, differences between different social groups, how changes in the NHS have had an impact on care, societal reaction to AIDS, how doctors see their role and position and mental health. Ask the students to report back regularly to make sure that they remain on task; asking them to produce interim reports. When completed, ask the students to produce a mini project – including a handout – outlining their findings and showing a critical awareness of the strengths and weaknesses of their chosen method.
Review learning	• Give an example of a quantitative and qualitative method. • Isolate one strength and one weakness of this method. • Give an example of this method being used in the sphere of health. • Explain one finding of your research. Does it back up or reject previous work in the area? • Why do you think that this is the case?
Preview next lesson	A mock exam on health.
End positively	Tell the students they've all worked really hard on this module.
What the examiners are looking for	In the sample material, questions on methods look at the strengths and weaknesses of two research methods. It is important that throughout the course that the inherent strengths and weaknesses of methodology are assessed.
Homework	Ask the students to revise this module ready for a health mock exam.
Getting the most out of your class	Why not get your class out to a university's sociology department? Higher education departments are often more than willing to allow what they consider prospective students to visit the university. Perhaps ask a few of the lecturers to explain what their present research is looking at. As ever, motivating your students remains a vital part of the educational process.

Sociological methods

Lesson One: Quantitative and qualitative methods of research

Topic	Group	Ability	No. of boys	No. of girls	No. of SEN	Teaching assistant
Quantitative and qualitative methods of research: an introduction.						

Start positive	Tell the students that you think they'll be very good at this module.
Connect learning	How you connect learning in this lesson depends on the order you teach the modules. If this is not the first module you will teach, ask questions on how certain sociologists came up with the theories covered in other topics.
Share learning objectives	• Understand how sociologists use different methods. • Understand the difference between quantitative and qualititative methodology. • Appreciate that whilst scientific experiments allow simple correlation even these observations are problematic.
Lesson outline	Looking at the methods that sociologists use.
Starter hook	Tell the students to imagine they have just decided that they would all like to become sociologists when they leave school. Ask them what they would do every day as part of their job? Ask the students to capture ideas on the whiteboard. The contributions should become progressively more sensible as you prompt the students and should end up with ideas such as 'interview people' and 'watch society'. Now introduce the notion of research methods.
Activity One	Use a slideshow or the overhead projector to introduce the reasons for sociological research. Specifically explain new terms such as 'subjectivity', 'objectivity', 'qualitative', 'quantitative', 'correlation', 'generalisation', 'empirical', 'validity' and 'reliability'. Explain that whilst some sociologists like to make up theories about a whole society, others prefer to do small-scale research on a particular social group.
Activity Two	Prepare a set of sticky notes, each containing one of the concepts learned in Activity One. Students should take it in turns to pick a note, without looking at the word, and stick it on their forehead. The rest of the class have to describe the word until the student wearing the sticky note guesses the answer.
Activity Three	Make a list of the main qualitative and quantitative research methods on the whiteboard. Ask the students to use a range of textbooks to make notes on each method in more detail.
Review learning	• What is correlation? • How far can we be sure that experiments are reliable? • List two quantitative research methods and two qualitative methods. • Define the terms 'objective' and 'subjective'.
Preview next lesson	Next lesson we look at some key concepts – specifically a 'hypothesis' and 'operationalise'.
End positively	Tell the students it was a really good start to the module.
What the examiners are looking for	Students should have a keen awareness of how theory and methods combine. They need to remain evaluative of methods used by sociologists.
Homework	Ask the students to create a research methods glossary containing the new terms learned.
Getting the most out of your class	A number of resources can be recommended such as *The Sociology Teaching Handbook* by Chris Middleton.

Lesson Two: Quantitative and qualitative methods of research

Topic	Group	Ability	No. of boys	No. of girls	No. of SEN	Teaching assistant
Research design and its limitations.						

Start positive	Tell the students they are learning these new concepts very quickly!
Connect learning	• What is correlation? • How far can we be sure that experiments are reliable? • Define the terms 'objective' and 'subjective'.
Share learning objectives	• Comprehend the concept of hypotheses. • Understand how hypotheses can be proved or disproved. • Be aware of the concept of operationalisation. • Understand the difficulties that occur when measuring concepts.
Lesson outline	Key concepts lesson; looking at the concepts of hypothesis and operationalisation.
Starter hook	Ask the students to look up the term 'hypothesis'. What does it mean?
Activity One	Split the students into groups of three and give them a number of propositions. Ask them to isolate what kind of evidence they would need to find to prove the supposition or hypothesis. Examples you could use include: • Female pupils do more homework than male pupils in secondary schools. • Crime increases when there is more unemployment. • Young people learn most of their attitudes from their peer group. • Suicide rates decrease during wartime.
Activity Two	Give the other groups five minutes to identify why the suggested evidence would not prove the statement. Summarise key problems raised with regard to concepts such as 'bias', 'subjectivity', 'representativeness', and so on. This allows students to draw upon knowledge gained in the previous lesson. Remind students that it is difficult to prove propositions as 'true'.
Activity Three	Using Jane Elliot's *Sociology Review* article, *What do women want?*, ask the students to list the factors that are likely to influence a person's choice of full-time or part-time work. Are the factors the same for males and females? Students should identify, with your assistance, the Hakim hypothesis and those aspects of it that require operationalising; for example, 'commitment', 'happy' with the traditional division of women and 'choice'. Set students the task of designing questions that might operationalise these concepts.
Review learning	• What is a hypothesis? Give an example. • How would you prove or disprove a hypothesis? • What does the term 'operationalise' mean? • Explain why it may be difficult to operationalise concepts.
Preview next lesson	Looking at quantitative and qualitative methodology.
End positively	Tell the students it was a really good lesson today.
What the examiners are looking for	The new AQA AS exam has three short answer questions that tend to require knowledge of a range of concepts such as covered in this lesson.
Homework	Ask the students to explore the school or college library. They should find out how many different textbooks and revision guides there are that deal with sociological methods. They should ask the librarian if they subscribe to *Sociology Review* or a different sociology magazine. Ask them to record their notes in their sociology journal.
Getting the most out of your class	With less exams being taken the board envisages that teachers will set mini projects for their students. You should set these on either education or health, as befits the AQA specification.

Lesson Three: Quantitative and qualitative methods of research

Topic	Group	Ability	No. of boys	No. of girls	No. of SEN	Teaching assistant
Sampling, pilot studies and primary research methods.						

Start positive	Tell the students it was a good introductory lesson last time.
Connect learning	<ul><li>Explain the terms 'qualititative' and 'qualitative'.</li><li>Which types of theory would use each of the above?</li><li>Give an advantage of using statistical data similar to the data used in the natural sciences.</li><li>Give one disadvantage of using this method.</li><li>Give an advantage of using qualitative data; for instance, a report on a theft taken from the actors themselves.</li><li>Give one disadvantage of using qualitative data.</li></ul>
Share learning objectives	<ul><li>Understand how theory and methods are interlinked.</li><li>Appreciate what makes a good questionnaire and what makes a poor one.</li><li>Understand how sampling is used within research.</li></ul>
Lesson outline	A general introduction as to how sociologists use methodology for research.
Starter hook	Ask the students to mix and match examples of primary and secondary types of research.
Activity One	Explain the importance of sampling. Give each student a numbered raffle ticket. Have three or four small prizes ready (pencils, chocolate bars, etc). Announce the winners by picking the numbers out of a hat. Through discussion, let the students relate this to random sampling in sociological research. First of all ask them to think where they could obtain a sampling frame for the following circumstances: voting behaviour, church attendance, child care problems of single-parent families, and so on. Now ask them to make notes on the main sampling methods (random, systematic, stratified, snowballing, etc).
Activity Two	Introduce the ideas of positivism and anti-positivism (interpretivism). Explain which methods would be used by each. Ask the students to produce a questionnaire. Topics they could look into include voting behaviour, what pupils think of their school and the domestic labour debate. Ask the students to produce ten questions to be answered by the respondents. Once these are completed pass them around groups and ask them to assess each questionnaire. This is best done with an assessment sheet. Ask them to feedback which questions they were happy with and which needed some work. Link this activity to the notion of pilot studies: what are they and why are they conducted?
Activity Three	Ask the students to produce a questionnaire with deliberate mistakes for the other students to spot or produce your own questionnaire with mistakes for the students to identify.
Activity Four	Produce a list of key concepts learned in the lesson and ask the students to mix and match them to their correct answers.
Review learning	<ul><li>What is positivism and anti-positivism (interpretivism)?</li><li>Give an example of a method what would be used by each.</li><li>What makes a good questionnaire?</li><li>Give an example of a sampling method.</li><li>Explain a key concept learnt in this lesson.</li></ul>
Preview next lesson	Looking at participant observation and its strengths and weaknesses.
End positively	Tell the students there were some great questionnaires produced today.
What the examiners are looking for	Examiners like to see that students are aware of how theory and methods are interlinked. This can be especially useful when it comes to evaluating research studies quoted in essays.
Homework	Ask the students to create a poster for wall display. They should include an explanation of positivism, anti-positivism (interpretivism) and the types of research methods they each use.
Getting the most out of your class	Try to ensure that you include activities, as well as just explaining. This helps kinetic learners in particular.

Lesson Four: Sources of data and their strengths and limitations

Topic	Group	Ability	No. of boys	No. of girls	No. of SEN	Teaching assistant
Experiments and social surveys.						

Start positive	Tell the students they showed a good understanding of sampling methods last lesson.
Connect learning	• What is positivism and anti-positivism (interpretivism)? • Give an example of a method what would be used by each. • What makes a good questionnaire? • Give an example of a sampling method. • Explain a key concept learnt last lesson.
Share learning objectives	• Explain the difference between lab and field experiments. • Analyse the strengths and weaknesses of both types of experiments. • Assess the advantages and disadvantages of questionnaires. • Explain how response rates can be improved.
Lesson outline	An assessment of the strengths and limitations of the main quantitative methods.
Starter hook	Ask students to work in pairs to try to define an experiment (this is harder than it sounds!).
Activity One	Provide a list of key terms associated with experiments on the whiteboard ('lab experiment', 'field experiment', 'variable', 'correlation', 'dependent variable', 'independent variable', and so on). Now give each student some blu tack and a card containing a definition of one of the terms. Students should place their card next to the correct term on the whiteboard. A handout with the correct answers could be provided afterwards.
Activity Two	Ask students to use a range of texts to find examples of sociological studies using lab or field experiments (remind them to use notes from previous modules such as Rosenthal and Jacobsen's study from *education*). Initiate a discussion about the usefulness of the experiment in sociology. Use questioning to prompt the students to link this to positivism.
Activity Three	Ask the students to create a table with four sections: advantages and disadvantages of lab experiments plus advantages and disadvantages of field experiments. Use a range of texts plus students' own ideas to complete the table (note key points that must be covered include ethics, controlling variables, validity and reliability).
Activity Four	Ask the students to find the questionnaires they devised last lesson and use these as a prompt to think of the advantages and disadvantages of postal questionnaires. These can be written as a simple list, using the textbook for help. Again, encourage them to use terms such as 'reliability', 'validity', 'response rates', and so on. Now create a spider diagram on the whiteboard containing students' ideas on how the response rate of questionnaires could be improved.
Review learning	• What are the two types of experiment called in sociology? • Which type has better validity? • How could each type be unethical? • Give three disadvantages of postal questionnaires.
Preview next lesson	Examining types of observation used in research.
End positively	Tell the students you're looking forward to reading their essays.
What the examiners are looking for	Students need to know at least three advantages and disadvantages of each research method. This will enable them to answer 20 mark questions in detail.
Homework	Set the students a mini-essay examining the problems sociologists may find when using participant observation in their research (300–500 words). Students may need a brief plan to help them. Remind them to look at the problems of overt and covert observation separately, and also include advantages to meet AO2 requirements.
Getting the most out of your class	Ask the students to give out copies of their questionnaires to other sixth form students and to monitor how many actually come back!

Lesson 5

Lesson Five: Sources of data

Topic	Group	Ability	No. of boys	No. of girls	No. of SEN	Teaching assistant
Longitudinal research.		AS				

Start positive	Tell the students it was an excellent lesson on experiments last time.
Connect learning	<ul><li>What are the two types of experiment called in sociology?</li><li>Which type has better validity?</li><li>How could each type be unethical?</li><li>Give three disadvantages of postal questionnaires.</li></ul>
Share learning objectives	<ul><li>Know examples of longitudinal research.</li><li>Understand the practicalities of this kind of research.</li><li>Be aware of the strengths and weaknesses of this technique.</li></ul>
Lesson outline	A look and assessment of longitudinal research.
Starter hook	Print out the following article and ask the students to think up some disadvantages of longitudinal surveys: http://news.bbc.co.uk/1/hi/education/705793.stm.
Activity One	Ask the students to visit the following web page: http://www.socialresearchmethods.net/tutorial/Cho2/cho1.html. Ask them to summarise the following concepts as they relate to longitudinal studies: trend studies, cohort studies and panel studies.
Activity Two	Ask the students to visit the following web page: http://www.iser.essex.ac.uk/ulsc/about/whatlong.php. Split the students into pairs and ask each of the groups to chose one of the following longitudinal surveys: *1970 British Cohort Study, British Household Panel Survey* (BHPS), *English Longitudinal Study of Ageing* (ELSA), *Families and Children Study and Millennium Cohort Study.* For each ask the students to answer the following: What was the rationale or reason for the study? Explain how sampling was used. What was included in the survey? Explain the results obtained.
Activity Three	Display a typical exam question on an overhead projector or whiteboard (for example, suggest one advantage and one disadvantage of longitudinal research). Ask students to discuss possible answers to this in pairs, and then take suggestions from each pair. Clarify the main points: that longitudinal research allows sociologists to study changes over time, but is time-consuming, costly and sample attrition could occur.
Review learning	<ul><li>What is a longitudinal study?</li><li>Explain the advantages and disadvantages of this technique.</li><li>Give an example of a longitudinal survey.</li><li>Why are these useful?</li></ul>
Preview next lesson	Looking at observation.
End positively	Tell the students they're doing very well in this module so far.
What the examiners are looking for	The examiners want students to appreciate that longitudinal research is not just a study 'over a long period of time', but one in which participants are surveyed at regular internals.
Homework	Ask students to make revision notes or mind maps on all of the research methods they've learned so far.
Getting the most out of your class	To incorporate an element of role play, why not host a 'sociology chat show'? Take the role of the host, giving each student a name tag (Oakley, Durkheim, James Patrick, and so on). The topic could be very general such as 'what research method is best for sociological research?' Let the students decide how the conversation develops!

Lesson Six: Sources of data and their strengths and limitations

Topic	Group	Ability	No. of boys	No. of girls	No. of SEN	Teaching assistant
Participant/non-participant observation.		AS				

Start positive	Tell the students it was an excellent lesson on questionnaires and the different methods used by sociologists last time.
Connect learning	• What is a longitudinal study? • Explain the advantages and disadvantages of this technique. • Give an example of a longitudinal survey. • Why are these useful?
Share learning objectives	• Distinguish between covert and overt participant observation. • Give examples of participant observation. • Evaluate observation and participant observation.
Lesson outline	An assessment of the strengths and limitations of observation.
Starter hook	Ask the students to write an account of the last lesson. Ask them to compare the accounts in pairs. Did the students pick out the same important events? Did the students know exactly what was happening? What were the main areas of agreement and disagreement? How can you use this knowledge to criticise participant observation?
Activity One	Ask the students how easy it would be to observe a number of differing groups (a family, a football crowd, a delinquent gang, prisoners, school teachers, nightclub goers, the cabinet and a board of directors). Give each a rating out of ten, with ten being the easiest.
Activity Two	Uses extracts from a number of bits of work and discuss them. Good examples include Bill Whyte's study (1993), *James Patrick* (1973), Laud Humphries (1970), Ned Polksy (1967), and so on. Discuss the advantages of the research and the weaknesses.
Activity Three	Ask the students to work in pairs to produce a presentation on a specific study. Ask the students to outline the research, what each study discovered, and the advantages and disadvantages; including the general strengths and weaknesses of observation.
Review learning	• Give an example of where participant observation is fairly easy. • Quote some examples of covert and overt observation. • Give one strength of this method and one weakness. • Exemplify this using a case study.
Preview next lesson	Examining types of interview used in research.
End positively	Tell the students you're looking forward to reading their essays.
What the examiners are looking for	Participant observation remains a popular 20 mark question.
Homework	Set the students a mini-essay: Examine the problems sociologists may find when using participant observation in their research (300–500 words). Students may need a brief plan to help them. Remind them to look at the problems of overt and covert observation separately, and also include advantages to meet AO2 requirements.
Getting the most out of your class	Why not get your students to do their own participant observation? This can be done observing one of your lessons, at the supermarket, at a football ground, and so on. Ask the students to produce their own pro formas to record what is happening. Ask them to report back their findings.

Lesson 7

Lesson Seven: Sources of data and their strengths and limitations

Topic	Group	Ability	No. of boys	No. of girls	No. of SEN	Teaching assistant
Interviews.		AS				

Start positive	Tell the students it was a good lesson participant and non-participant observation last time.
Connect learning	<ul><li>Give an example of where participant observation is fairly easy.</li><li>Quote some examples of covert and overt observation.</li><li>Give one strength of this method and one weakness.</li><li>Exemplify this using a case study.</li></ul>
Share learning objectives	<ul><li>Understand the difference between structured and unstructured interviews.</li><li>Quote examples of such research.</li><li>Understand the advantages and disadvantages of each technique.</li><li>Understand these issues as a result of interviewing each other.</li></ul>
Lesson outline	Assessing structured and unstructured interviews.
Starter hook	Ask the students to tell you which interview method would be used by a positivist or an anti-positivist (interpretivist).
Activity One	Divide the students into pairs. Ask them to sit with a person they do not usually sit next to. Ask one student in the pair should be the interviewer; the other the interviewee. Ask them to conduct an informal interview (lasting 10 minutes) why the interviewee chose the A levels they did, and whether they are enjoying them. The interviewer should initiate the conversation, but then should listen; only prompting to clarify points when necessary. All interviewers should take notes. After 10 minutes each pair is to complete Activity Two.
Activity Two	Ask the students if they felt comfortable in revealing the reasons for their choice of A levels. Did they like the fact that their responses were being recorded? Did knowing the interviewer make it easier or more difficult to be honest? Were their answers a true reflection of the reason why they chose their A levels? What did they dislike about the interview? Was it difficult to question someone who they knew? Did they have to prompt the interviewee? How much of the material that was gained was useful? Now introduce the advantages and disadvantages of both structured and unstructured interviews. Stress the point that interviewer bias could occur in both types of interview.
Activity Three	Consider a range of circumstances when interviewer bias might occur. For example, a white person being questioned by a black person about their racial attitudes, an adult interviewing students in a school, a British person interviewing a French person about their attitudes to the English, and so on. Ask the students to think up some of their own examples.
Review learning	<ul><li>What is a structured interview?</li><li>Explain the difference between a structured interview and an unstructured interview.</li><li>Give an example of research that has been used in either of these interview techniques.</li><li>Explain an advantage and a disadvantage of each interview technique.</li></ul>
Preview next lesson	Examining the use of official statistics.
End positively	Tell the students there were some good points on interviewer bias raised by X.
What the examiners are looking for	Students will be asked to use a stimulus item to apply their knowledge and understanding of sociological research methods as it applies to either education or health. Interviews, either unstructured or structured, are always likely to appear as a method for assessment.
Homework	Ask the students to use their textbooks or notes from other modules to find a sociological study that used interviews. Ask them to provide a brief summary of the study and state the advantages and disadvantages of using interviews for that particular study.
Getting the most out of your class	Why not ask a professional interviewer to talk to your sociology group? Given the wide range of organisations that use this technique it should be easy to obtain someone who will give your students a real appreciation of the demands of interviews.

Topic 6: Sociological methods

Lesson Eight: Sources of data and their strengths and limitations

Topic	Group	Ability	No. of boys	No. of girls	No. of SEN	Teaching assistant
Official statistics.		AS				

Start positive	Tell the students it was an excellent lesson on the different types of interview last time.
Connect learning	• What is a structured interview? • Explain the difference between a structured interview and an unstructured interview. • Give an example of research that has been used in either of these interview techniques. • Explain an advantage and a disadvantage of each interview technique.
Share learning objectives	• Understand the difference between official and unofficial statistics. • Quote examples of official and unofficial statistics. • Know which agencies publish this data. Evaluate their use.
Lesson outline	Looking at the use and the strengths and weaknesses of official statistics.
Starter hook	Get students to complete the 2001 census form (http://www.statistics.gov.uk/census2001/censusform.asp). Ask the students to make a list of the questions that they found difficult to answer or understand. Then ask them to make a list of any questions that they would have included in addition to what was included.
Activity One	Ensure students are confident in explaining the difference between primary and secondary data. Ask them to add these concepts to their glossary if needed. Now provide a list of the main secondary sources used by sociologists (official stats, life documents, historical documents, mass media and existing sociological studies). Explain that this lesson will focus solely on official statistics. Give the students a list of all the major surveys that are undertaken by the government. Include surveys such as the census, *General Household Survey*, *Family Expenditure Survey*, *National Food Survey*, *British Household Panel Survey*, *British Crime Survey*, and so on. Then ask the students to mix and match under which circumstances each would be used by sociologists.
Activity Two	Ask the students to produce a presentation on each of the above types of official statistics. Perhaps widen the choice, by adding social trends, unemployment rates by month, and so on. Ask the students to explain how they are collected, the advantages and disadvantages of each when used by sociologists, which groups might be missed by the survey, what anti-positivists (interpretivists) and Marxists might say about the data, and so on.
Activity Three	Ask the students to download social trends (http://www.statistics.gov.uk/statbase/Product.asp?vlnk = 5748&More = N). Ask them to pick an area such as population, households and family, education, and so on. For each ask the students to isolate the major trends apparent for each. If you can, ask them to link back to other areas that have been studied.
Review learning	• Explain the difference between official and unofficial statistics. • Why should we be 'wary' of official statistics? • Give one advantage of using such data? • Given one disadvantage of using official statistics.
Preview next lesson	Looking at secondary sources.
End positively	Tell the students they gave excellent presentations today.
What the examiners are looking for	The idea of official statistics links really well with theory. Examiners like to see that students have sociological imagination. How, for example, do feminists, Marxists and interactionists see such data?
Homework	Ask the students to update their sociological methods glossary to include all the new terms learned recently.
Getting the most out of your class	It is always a good idea to set regular tasks for your students. Official statistics can be obtained easily on the Internet as part of a homework task.

Lesson
9

Lesson Nine: Sources of data and their strengths and limitations

Topic	Group	Ability	No. of boys	No. of girls	No. of SEN	Teaching assistant
Secondary sources.		AS				

Start positive	Tell the students they showed a good understanding of official statistics last lesson.
Connect learning	<ul><li>Explain the difference between primary and secondary data.</li><li>Explain the difference between official and unofficial statistics.</li><li>Why should we be 'wary' of official statistics?</li><li>Give one advantage of using such data.</li><li>Given one disadvantage of using official statistics.</li></ul>
Share learning objectives	<ul><li>List all the secondary sources used by sociologists.</li><li>Assess the usefulness of each type.</li><li>Apply John Scott's criteria to each source.</li></ul>
Lesson outline	An assessment of the strengths and limitations of different secondary sources.
Starter hook	Hide a set of cards around the room before the lesson starts. The cards should contain either a type of secondary source (media, historical, life, and so on) or a definition of one of these. Ask the students to each find a card and then find the person who has the definition to their term (or vice versa).
Activity One	Provide a handout detailing the sources and their definitions from the starter hook activity. Explain to students that they may get an exam just on official statistics, or it may be a question on secondary data in general.
Activity Two	Ask the students to work in pairs or small groups to research the strengths and weaknesses of one type of secondary source from the handout. To extend this task, give each group the name of a sociologist who used the source and ask them to research their study (for example, use Ariès from the *families* module for historical documents, Valerie Hey from *education* for life documents, and so on).
Activity Three	Ask each group to present their findings to the class.
Activity Four	On a handout or presentation, introduce John Scott's criteria for checking secondary sources (students may need definitions of authenticity and credibility). Initiate a discussion on which types of secondary sources are authentic, credible, represenive, and so on.
Review learning	<ul><li>Explain what is meant by secondary data.</li><li>List four secondary sources.</li><li>Give two disadvantages of using official statistics.</li><li>Comment on the validity of personal and life documents.</li><li>What are the four criteria for assessing secondary sources according to Scott?</li></ul>
Preview next lesson	Drawing together everything learned on positivism and anti-positivism (interpretivism).
End positively	Tell the students it was a really good lesson on the strengths and limitations of different secondary sources today.
What the examiners are looking for	Students need to assess the usefulness of secondary data both as whole, but also as individual sources.
Homework	Ask the students to design a poster showing the strengths and weaknesses of secondary data. They should include reference to John Scott.
Getting the most out of your class	When doing group work, strike a balance between letting students work with their friends and mixing them up. Names of each group can be pulled out of a hat.

Lesson Ten: The relationship between positivism, anti-positivism (interpretivism) and sociological methods

Topic	Group	Ability	No. of boys	No. of girls	No. of SEN	Teaching assistant
Positivism and anti-positivism (interpretivism).		AS				

Start positive	Tell the students they showed a good understanding of sampling methods last lesson.
Connect learning	• What is positivism? • Name two positivists. • What is anti-positivism (interpretivism)? • What research methods do positivists like to use? • What research methods do interpretivists like to use?
Share learning objectives	• Revise existing knowledge of positivism and anti-positivism (interpretivism). • Revise which research methods are used by positivists and interpretivists. • Apply this knowledge to the debate on whether sociology is a science.
Lesson outline	An assessment of the strengths and limitations of the main quantitative methods.
Starter hook	Ask students to work in pairs to discuss the question 'what is science'?
Activity One	Ask the students to name some science subjects: capture these on the whiteboard. Now ask them if sociology is a science. Does it fit the definitions they discussed? Now provide a clear definition of science; for example, Giddens' definition. Again, ask students if sociology does the things that science does.
Activity Two	Draw together everything students have already learned about positivism. This is a good opportunity to revise key terms. Ask then to define 'experiment', 'correlation', 'variables', 'objectivity' and 'empiricism'. Stress the point that positivists believe sociology to be a science that produces social facts.
Activity Three	Now do the same for anti-positivism (interpretivism). Revise the qualitative research methods and ask students to explain 'subjectivity', 'validity' and 'free will'. Stress the point that interpretivists would say that sociology is not a science, nor should it be one. Revise the criticisms of experiments and social surveys, and ask students whether these 'scientific' methods really produce facts.
Activity Four	As a plenary, borrow some university prospectuses from the careers office or library. Ask the students to find details of sociology degrees and explain the difference between a BA and BSc. Is sociology regarded as a science by universities? Does this have implications for the prestige of the subject?
Review learning	• Define the term 'science'. • Name one sociologist that would say sociology is scientific. • List two methods considered as scientific by positivists. • Name one sociologist that would say sociology is not scientific. • Describe some flaws of quantitative methods to support this claim.
Preview next lesson	Looking at what influences sociologists when choosing their topic and research methods.
End positively	Tell the students they demonstrated really impressive knowledge today.
What the examiners are looking for	Students need to apply positivist and interpretivist views to each research method covered.
Homework	Ask the students to update their sociology glossaries as they are nearly at the end of the module.
Getting the most out of your class	Ask the students in advance of the lesson to take on a persona of a positivist or an interpretivist that they keep up for the duration of the lesson (they could even dress like Durkheim, Weber, and so on!).

**Lesson
11**

Lesson Eleven: Theoretical, practical and ethical considerations

Topic	Group	Ability	No. of boys	No. of girls	No. of SEN	Teaching assistant
The theoretical, practical and ethical considerations influencing the choice of topic, choice of method(s) and the conduct of research.		AS				

Start positive	Tell the students it was a great debate last lesson.
Connect learning	• Define the term 'science'. • Name one sociologist that would say sociology is scientific. • List two methods considered as scientific by positivists. • Name one sociologist that would say sociology is not scientific. • Describe some flaws of quantitative methods to support this claim.
Share learning objectives	For students to be aware of practical and ethical considerations as they apply to sociological research, and be able to quote examples of research studies that either show high ethical concern or low levels of ethics.
Lesson outline	Assessing the importance of ethics when doing social research and consider examples of good and poor practice.
Starter hook	Brainstorm what practical and ethical considerations might occur when doing sociological research. Ask the students to write these on the whiteboard.
Activity One	Give the students clear definitions of 'theoretical considerations' (draw upon their knowledge of positivism and anti-positivism [interpretivism]), practical considerations and ethical considerations. Initiate a discussion on which of these are most important when researching.
Activity Two	Split students into pairs. Then give each pair a pack of material that relates to one specific piece of research. Studies that could be used include: Paul Willis' *Learning to Labour* (1977), Laud Humphrey's *The Tearoom Trade* (1970), James Patrick's *A Glasgow Gang Observed* (1973), Rosenthal and Jacobsen's *Pygmalion in the Classroom* (1968), Dunning et al., *The Roots of Football Hooliganism* (1989) and finally, Eileen Barker's *Making of a Moonie* (1984). Ask each group to explain how the researchers chose to do their research, the findings obtained, and how practical and ethical considerations had impacted on the research.
Activity Three	Look at the following: http://www.socresonline.org.uk/info/ethguide.html or www.sociology.org.uk/as4bsoce.pdf. From the guidelines, ask your students in groups to produce a poster of ethical conduct that should be followed by all social researchers. Ask each group to present their poster. Do they agree with all of them?
Review learning	• Explain the term 'ethical'. • Give an example of how a research study could be unethical. • Quote an example. • Why might ethics get in the way of sociological research?
Preview next lesson	The next lesson draws the entire module together.
End positively	Tell the students it was another really productive lesson.
What the examiners are looking for	Examiners like to ask questions in which students decide which of the practical, theoretical and ethical considerations are most influential in social research. This means they need to refer to a range of studies where these considerations were taken into account.
Homework	Ask the students to revise all of the module so far in preparation for a mini test.
Getting the most out of your class	Why not invest in a magnetic dart board to hang on the classroom wall? This gives an exciting twist to the traditional team quiz. Split the students into teams. Ask the first team a question and if they answer correctly, one team member throws a dart. Their score is the number of points they win for their team.

Lesson Twelve: Durkheim's study of suicide: bringing it all together

Topic	Group	Ability	No. of boys	No. of girls	No. of SEN	Teaching assistant
Quantitative and qualitative methods of research, their strengths and limitations; research design.		AS				

Start positive	Tell the students they've all worked really hard on this module.
Connect learning	• Explain the term 'ethical'. • Give an example of how a research study could be unethical. • Quote an example. • Why might ethics get in the way of sociological research?
Share learning objectives	• Assess why people commit suicide. • Understand the importance of Durkheim's scientific methodology. • Be aware of the reasons why Durkheim considered suicide rates to vary within Europe. • Understand and apply Durkheim's different suicide categories.
Lesson outline	An assessment of Durkheim's study of suicide.
Starter hook	Have a set of sticky notes or cards hidden in various parts of the classroom. Ask each student to find a card or sticky note, which should have a question on it on anything covered in the module, and answer the question correctly.
Activity One	Ask the students to do some research on suicide in other cultures. For instance, ask them to look at suttee, hara-kiri and kamikaze. Investigate how these cultures view suicide.
Activity Two	Construct a quiz called 'How much do you know about suicide?' Ask the students to assess whether the following are true or false: • There were 5554 suicides in the United Kingdom in 2004. • Friday is the most common day for people to commit suicide in England and Wales. • Suicide trends over the last 10 years show a 9.5 per cent decrease in the UK overall. • Males between the ages of 25–34 are three times as likely to kill themselves as females of the same age group. • Suicide is now the forth most common cause of death amongst young people (http://www.samaritans.org/about_samaritans/facts_and_figures/facts_about_suicide.aspx).
Activity Three	Introduce Durkheim's study, drawing together concepts learned in this module (objectivity, hypothesis, official statistics, positivism, social facts, secondary data and quantitative data can all be drawn out here!) Give a few instances of different suicides and then ask students to link each to one of Durkheim's suicide types.
Review learning	• Define suicide. • Why is it difficult to do this? • Explain the methodology used by Durkheim. • What is social integration? • Give an example of each type of suicide as specified by Durkheim.
Preview next lesson	Mock exam time!
End positively	Tell the students they done well in now being able to fuse all their knowledge in an assessment of Durkheim's important study on suicide.
What the examiners are looking for	Durkheim's study of suicide offers an excellent way for examiners to assess whether students understand the differences between positivist and anti-positivist (interpretivist) theory.
Homework	Mini essay: Assess the usefulness of quantitative and qualitative sources of data in studying suicide.
Getting the most out of your class	You can use contemporary news to look at suicide. For instance, ask the students to look at the work of Dignitas (http://news.bbc.co.uk/1/hi/health/1958414.stm).

Bibliography

1901 Census Online, http://www.1901censusonline.com/ (Accessed 7 August 2007).

1970 British Cohort Study, Centre for Longitudinal Studies (BCS70).

Ansley, C., *The Growth and Structure of Human Populations: A Mathematical Investigation* (Princeton University Press, 1972).

AQA Sociology, www.aqa.org.uk (Accessed 7 March 2008).

AQA, *Access to Scripts*, http://www.aqa.org.uk/admin/p_results_access.php

Arber, S., and Cooper, H., 'Gender differences in health in later life: the new paradox?' *Social Science and Medicine* (Elsevier, 1999).

Banks, J., Breeze, E., Lessof, C., Nazroo, J., *Living in the 21st century: older people in England*, The 2006 English Longitudinal Study of Ageing (ELSA), (Institute for Fiscal Studies, 2006).

Barker, E., *The Making of a Moonie: Choice or Brainwashing?* (Blackwell, 1984).

Batty, D., *Exorcism: abuse or cure?*, http://www.guardian.co.uk/society/2001/may/02/socialcare.mentalhealth1 (2 May 2001), (Accessed 4 February 2008).

BBC News, *Why did Reg Crew want to die?*, http://news.bbc.co.uk/1/hi/health/1958414.stm (20 January 2003), (Accessed 6 July 2007).

BBC online, *The Surgery, Homophobia: What is it?*, http://www.bbc.co.uk/surgery/your_world/bullying/homophobia/ (Accessed 17 July 2007).

BBC, *Doctor defends IVF for woman*, 62, http://news.bbc.co.uk/1/hi/health/4971930.stm (Accessed 2 February 2008).

BBC, *How old do you have to be?*, http://news.bbc.co.uk/cbbcnews/hi/quiz/newsid_1855000/1855899.stm (Accessed 7 July 2007).

BBC, *Legal Ages Quiz Sheet*, http://news.bbc.co.uk/cbbcnews/hi/newsid_3190000/newsid_3190400/3190448.stm (Accessed 3 April 2007).

BBC, *Study team hunts 30-somethings*, http://news.bbc.co.uk/1/hi/education/705793.stm (8 April 2000), Accessed 3 April 2008).

Brassed Off (Channel Four Films, 1996).

British Sociological Association, *Statement of Ethical Practice for the British Sociological Association*, www.sociology.org.uk/as4bsoce.pdf (March 2002),(Accessed 8 July 2007).

Browne, K., and Bottrill, I., 'Unequal Unhealthy Nation', *Sociology Review* (Philip Allen Publishers, November 1999).

Bupa, www.bupa.co.uk (Accessed 2 September 2007).

Butler, P., *Q&A: Postcode lottery*, http://www.guardian.co.uk/society/2000/nov/09/NHS (*Guardian*, 9 November 2000), (Accessed 7 March 2008).

Cabinet Office, http://www.cabinetoffice.gov.uk/ (Accessed 3 April 2008).

Chester, R., *Divorce* in *The Sociology of Modern Britain*, Butterworth, E., and Weir, D., rev. edn. (Glasgow: Fontana, 1985).

Connexions, *Are You Old Enough?*, http://www.connexions-somerset.org.uk/rights/areyouoldenough.html (Accessed 30 June 2008).

Davey Smith, G., Dorling, D., Shaw, M., *Health inequalities and New Labour: how the promises compare with real progress*, http://www.bmj.com/cgi/content/full/330/7498/1016 (Accessed 7 March 2008).

Davidson, N., Townsend, P., and Whitehead, M., *Inequalities in Health*, www.scotpho.org.uk/nmsruntime/saveasdialog.asp?lID = 1057&sID = 1655, 1992 Edition, (Accessed 7 March 2008).

Department for Environment Food and Rural Affairs, *National Food Survey*, https://statistics.defra.gov.uk/esg/publications/nfs/default.asp (Accessed 7 March 2008).

Directgov, *Definition of 'disability' under the Disability Discrimination Act (DDA)*, http://www.direct.gov.uk/en/DisabledPeople/RightsAndObligations/DisabilityRights/DG_4001069 (Accessed 3 August 2007).

Directgov, *Disability rights*, http://www.direct.gov.uk/en/DisabledPeople/RightsAndObligations/DisabilityRights/index.htm (Accessed 5 March 2008).

Directgov, *Maternity, paternity and adoption rights*, http://www.direct.gov.uk/en/Diol1/EmploymentInteractiveTools/DG_065384 (Accessed 3 December 2007).

Directgov, *What are tax credits?*, http://www.direct.gov.uk/en/MoneyTaxAndBenefits/TaxCreditsandChildBenefit/TaxCredits/DG_073802 (Accessed 2 December 2007).

Dunning, E., Murphy, P., and Williams, J., *The Roots of Football Hooliganism* (London: Routledge and Kegan Paul, 1989).

Dunscombe, J., and Marsden, D., 'Love and intimacy: The gender division of emotion and emotion work', *Sociology* 27 (2), (1993), pp. 221–42.

Durkheim, È., *Suicide* (New York: Free Press, 1951).

East is East (Film Four, 1999).

Edgell, S., *Middle Class Couples* (London: Allen and Unwin, 1980).

Education Forum, *History of Education in the UK 1870-1965, Gap-fill exercise*, http://www.educationforum.co.uk/sociology_2/historyeducation.htm (Accessed 3 September 2007).

Education Forum, *History of Education in the UK 1870–1965*, http://www.educationforum.co.uk/sociology_2/historyeducation.htm (Accessed 5 February 2008).

Eleven plus exams, *Heads for Success*, www.elevenplusexams.co.uk/ (Accessed 4 February 2008).

Elliot, J., 'What do women want?' *Sociology Review*, Vol.6 (7), (Philip Allen Publishers, April 1997), pp. 12–14.

Equality and Human Rights Commission, *Equality and Human Rights*, www.equalityhumanrights.com/ (Accessed 3 September 2007).

European Socio-economic Classification, http://www.iser.essex.ac.uk/esec/guide/descriptions.php (Accessed 7 October 2007).

Eversley, D., and Bonnerjea, L., *Social Change and Indicators of Diversity* in *Families in Britain*, Rapoport, R., Fogarty, M., and Rapoport, R., eds. (London: Kegan Paul, 1982).

Gans, H., *The functions of poverty* in *Social Problems of the Modern World*, (Wadsworth Publishing, January 2000), pp. 34–8.

Garrod, J., Williams, J., eds., *Sociology Review* (Philip Allen Publishers, November 1999).

Gender and Health Collaborative Curriculum Project, *Gender and Depression*, http://www.genderandhealth.ca/en/modules/depression/depression-impact-and-incidence-04.jsp (Accessed 22 December 2007).

General Medical Council, http://www.gmc-uk.org/ (Accessed 6 January 2008).

Gingerbread, http://www.gingerbread.org.uk/ (Accessed 14 June 2007).

Gordon, D., Adelman, L., Ashworth, K., Bradshaw J., Levitas, R., Middleton, S., Pantazis,C., Patsios, D., Payne, S., Townsend, P., and Williams, J., *Poverty and social exclusion in Britain*, http://www.jrf.org.uk/knowledge/findings/socialpolicy/930.asp (Joseph Rowntree Foundation, 2000), (Accessed 3 January 2008).

Gordon, D., Adelman, L., Ashworth, K., Bradshaw J., Levitas, R., Middleton, S., Pantazis, C., Patsios, D., Payne, S., Townsend, P., and Williams, J., *Poverty and social exclusion in Britain*, http://www.jrf.org.uk/knowledge/findings/socialpolicy/930.asp (Joseph Rowntree Foundation, 2000), (Accessed 7 June 2007).

Hey, V., 'Dancing Round Handbags, Young Women's friendships as sites of solidarity and struggle', *Journal Ex aequo*, Celta Editora, 7 (2003), pp. 49–69.

HM Revenue and Customs, *National Minimum Wage*, http://www.hmrc.gov.uk/nmw/

HM Revenue and Customs, *Personal Wealth*, http://www.hmrc.gov.uk/stats/personal_wealth/table13_5.pdf (Accessed 4 February 2008).

Home Office, Crime in England and Wales 2006/2007 (Crown Copyright, 2006).

http://www.direct.gov.uk (Accessed 14 February 2008).

Humphreys, L., *The Tearoom Trade, Impersonal Sex in Public Places* (London: Duckworth, 1970).

Kan, M. Y., 'Work Orientation and Wives' Employment Careers: an evaluation of Hakim's preference theory', *Work and Occupations* 34 (4), (November 2007), pp. 430–62.

Kelly, A., *Science for Girls* (Milton Keynes: Open Uiversity Press, 1987).

Laing, R. D., *The Obvious* in *The Dialectics of Liberation*, Cooper, D., ed. (Harmondsworth: Penguin, 1971).

Lawson T., Jones, M., Moores, R., *Advanced Sociology through Diagrams* (Oxford University Press, 2000).

Lawson, T., Moores, R., and Jones, M., *AS and A level Sociology Through Diagrams* (Oxford University Press, 2000).

Longitudinal Research, http://www.socialresearchmethods.net/tutorial/Cho2/cho1.html (Accessed 16 April 2008).

Lyon, N., Barnes, M., and Sweiry, D., *Families with Children in Britain: Findings from the 2004 Families and Children Survey* (Department of Work and Pensions, 2006).

Make Poverty History, http://www.makepovertyhistory.org/ (Accessed 22 December 2007).

Marxists Internet Archive, *Marx/Engles Image Library*, http://www.marxists.org/archive/marx/photo/index.htm (Accessed 8 July 2007).

Middleton, C., *Sociology Teaching Handbook* (Sheffield University, 1993).

Murray, C., *Charles Murray and the Underclass: The Developing Debate*, www.civitas.org.uk/pdf/cw33.pdf, (The Institute of Economic Affairs Unit in association with the *Sunday Times*, London, 1996), (Accessed 2 September 2007).

Murray, C., with commentary by Phillips, M., *Charles Murray and the British Underclass 1990–2000*, www.civitas.org.uk/pdf/cs10.pdf (Trowbridge: Cromwell Press, February 2001).

My Masterclasses, http://www.a-grades.com/ (Accessed 3 March 2008).

NHS, www.nhs.uk (Accessed 2 September 2007).

Oakley, A., *Becoming a Mother* (Oxford: Martin Robertson), under the title *From Here to Maternity* (Harmondsworth: Penguin, 1979).

Office for National Statistics, *British Household Panel Survey* (British Household Panel Survey, 1991–2006).

Office for National Statistics, *Census Form*, http://www.statistics.gov.uk/census2001/censusform.asp (Accessed 4 April 2008).

Office for National Statistics, *Detailed category descriptions and operational issues*, http://www.statistics.gov.uk/methods_quality/ns_sec/cat_desc_op_issue.asp (Accessed 2 September 2007).

Office for National Statistics, *Detailed category descriptions and operational issues*, http://www.statistics.gov.uk/methods_quality/ns_sec/cat_desc_op_issue.asp (Accessed 3 June 2007).

Office for National Statistics, *Family Expenditure Survey* (Crown, 2005).

Office for National Statistics, *General Household Survey*, *Living in Britain* (Crown, 2005).

Office for National Statistics, *Living in Britain, General Household Survey*, http://www.statistics.gov.uk/ssd/surveys/general_household_survey.asp, (Crown, 2004), (Accessed 3 March 2008).

Office for National Statistics, *Social Trends 37* (Accessed 3 June 2007). http://www.statistics.gov.uk/downloads/theme_social/Social_Trends37/Social_Trends_37.pdf (2007).

Office for National Statistics, *Social Trends 37*, http://www.statistics.gov.uk/StatBase/Product.asp?vlnk = 5748 (2007), (Accessed 3 April 2008).

Ofsted, http://www.ofsted.gov.uk/ (Accessed 5 November 2007).

One Flew Over the Cuckoo's Nest (Fantasy Films, 1975).

One Parent Families, http://www.oneparentfamilies.org.uk/ (Accessed 20 June 2007).

One Parent Family Association, http://www.opfa.net/ (Accessed 15 June 2007).

Pahl, J., and Vogler, C., *Social and economic change and the organisation of money within marriage* (National Institute for Social Work, 1993).

Patrick, J., *A Glasgow Gang Observed*, (London: Methuen, 1973).

Philip Allan Updates, http://www.philipallan.co.uk/content.aspx?page = HOME (Accessed 8 March 2007).

Polksy, N., *Hustler Beats and Others* (Chicago: Aldine Publishing Co., 1967).

Postman, N., *Amusing ourselves to death* (Methuen, 1985).

Quality Trading, *Young Girl and Old Woman Optical Illusion*, http://www.qualitytrading.com/illusions/girlwoman.html (Accessed 4 March 2008).

Randhawa, G., *Tackling Health Inequalities for Ethnic Minority Groups: Challenges and Opportunities*, http://www.raceequalityfoundation.org.uk/hsc/files/health-brief6.pdf (Race Equality Foundation, 2007), (Accessed 7 March 2008).

Rapoport, R., Rapoport, R., and Streilitz, *Mothers, Fathers and Society: Towards New Alliances* (New York: Basic Books, 1977).

Rosenthal, R., and Jacobsen, L., *Pygmalion in the Classroom*, (New York: Rinehart and Winston, 1968).

Samaritans, *Facts about Suicide*, http://www.samaritans.org/about_samaritans/facts_and_figures/facts_about_suicide.aspx (Accessed 6 March 2008).

Sharpe, S., *Just Like a Girl: How Girls learn to be Women* (Penguin, 1994).

Sixth Sense, *Marxism*, http://sixthsense.osfc.ac.uk/sociology/as_sociology/marxism.asp (Accessed 4 July 2007).

SureStart, *SureStart Magazine*, http://www.surestart.gov.uk/magazine/ (Accessed 2 December 2007).

Taylor, P., et al., *Investigating Culture and Identity* (London: Collins Educational, 1997), p. 125.

The ESRC United Kingdom Longitudinal Studies Centre, *What are longitudinal studies?*, http://www.iser.essex.ac.uk/ulsc/about/whatlong.php (Accessed 16 April 2008).

The Full Monty (Redwave Films, 1997).

The Information Network, http://www.theinformationnet.com/ (Accessed 13 February 2008).

The Scottish Parliament, http://www.scottish.parliament.uk/vli/education/docs/enviro-studies/Debate/Duties_of_Members_of_the_Groups.pdf (Accessed 3 June 2007).

Times Online, 2008 *Rich List Search*, http://business.timesonline.co.uk/tol/business/specials/rich_list/rich_list_search/ (Accessed 3 January 2008).

Times online, *2008 Rich List Search*, http://business.timesonline.co.uk/tol/business/specials/rich_list/rich_list_search/ (Accessed 7 June 2007).

Times Online, *Sunday Times Rich List 2008 interactive table*, http://business.timesonline.co.uk/tol/business/specials/rich_list/?CMP = KNC-IX7429721604&HBX_PK = times + rich + list&HBX_OU = 50 (Accessed 5 February 2008).

Townsend Centre for International Poverty, http://www.bristol.ac.uk/poverty/news.html (Accessed 4 July 2007).

Tribal, *Network Training*, http://www.network-training.ac.uk/ (Accessed 3 December 2007).

UK Statistics Authority, *The UK Statistics Authority serves the public by promoting and safeguarding the quality of official statistics in the UK*, www.statistics.gov.uk (Accessed 2 February 2008).

Whyte, W. F., *Street Corner Society: The Social Structure of an Italian Slum* (University of Chicago Press, 1993).

Willis, P., *Learning to Labour* (Adershot: Gower, 1977).

Willmott, P., and Young, M., *Family and Kinship in East London* (Routledge and Kegan Paul, 1957).

World Health Organisation, *WHO definition of Health*, http://www.who.int/about/definition/en/print.html (Accessed 3 March 2008).

World Health Organisation, *WHO definition of Health*, http://www.who.int/about/definition/en/print.html (Accessed 3 August 2007).

Zaretsky, E., *Capitalism, the Family & Personal Life* (State and Revolution Series), (Harper & Row, 1976).